THE *ANNALS* OF FLODOARD OF REIMS,

9 1 9 - 9 6 6

D1598332

READINGS IN MEDIEVAL CIVILIZATIONS AND CULTURES: IX
series editor: Paul Edward Dutton

THE *ANNALS* OF FLODOARD OF REIMS,
919-966

edited and translated by

STEVEN FANNING & BERNARD S. BACHRACH

www.utphighereducation.com

Previously published by Broadview Press, © 2004 Steven Fanning and Bernard S. Bachrach

LIBRARY AND ARCHIVES CANADA CATALOGUING IN PUBLICATION

Flodoard, of Reims, 894–966
   The annals of Flodoard of Reims, 919–966 / edited and translated by Steven Fanning and Bernard S. Bachrach.

(Readings in medieval civilizations and cultures ; 9)
Index includes bibliographical references and index.

ISBN 978-1-44260-001-0

   1. France—History—To 987—Sources. I. Fanning, Steven II. Bachrach, Bernard S., 1939– III. Title. IV. Series.

DC70.A3F5813   2004   944'.014   C2004-904182-7

We welcome comments and suggestions regarding any aspect of our publications—please feel free to contact us at news@utphighereducation.com or visit our Internet site at www.utphighereducation.com.

North America
5201 Dufferin Street
North York, Ontario, Canada, M3H 5T8

2250 Military Road
Tonawanda, New York, USA, 14150

ORDERS PHONE: 1-800-565-9523
ORDERS FAX: 1-800-221-9985
ORDERS E-MAIL: utpbooks@utpress.utoronto.ca

UK, Ireland, and continental Europe
NBN International
Estover Road, Plymouth, PL6 7PY, UK
ORDERS PHONE: 44 (0) 1752 202301
ORDERS FAX: 44 (0) 1752 202333
ORDERS E-MAIL: enquiries@nbninternational.com

The University of Toronto Press acknowledges the financial support for its publishing activities of the Government of Canada through the Canada Book Fund.

Text design and composition by George Kirkpatrick

CONTENTS

LIST OF FIGURES

LIST OF MAPS

LIST OF GENEALOGIES

INTRODUCTION

Reims and the *Annals* of Flodoard

Tenth-century western Europe is famous for its paucity of narrative sources, or as it has been put, "The tenth century is very ill-served."[1] The great ninth-century annals, such as *The Annals of St. Bertin*, *Annals of Fulda*, *Annals of St. Vaast*, and the *Chronicle* of Regino of Prüm all draw to a close in the latter part of the century with few successors to carry on their historical accounts. Yet the tenth century saw a number of significant changes in western Europe. In the West Frankish kingdom, the monarchy was contested by the Carolingian and Robertian families, culminating in the accession of Hugh Capet in 987 and the establishment of the long-lasting Capetian dynasty. The last Viking raids afflicted the northwest of the kingdom and the nucleus of the duchy of Normandy was established at Rouen. In the eastern Frankish kingdom, the Carolingian dynasty failed due to lack of heirs and the powerful Saxon dynasty was established by Henry I, whose son and successor, Otto I, also gained the Italian throne and renewed the Western imperial title, thus creating the medieval German empire. Western Europe continued to be disrupted by raids of Saracens in Italy and southern Gaul, while the Magyars, newly arrived in Central Europe, conducted wide-ranging raids throughout the region.

One of the great exceptions to the generally bleak historical record of the tenth century is the priest Flodoard of Reims, whose *Annals* and *History of the Church of Reims* provide precious information on many of the major events of the mid-tenth century. Moreover, the *Annals* were used as one of the bases for the *History* written by one of the other principal tenth-century historians, Richer of Reims. Thus Flodoard's *Annals* stand as one of the essential narratives for a period poorly understood and lacking in detailed sources.

As Rosamond McKitterick wrote concerning the position of Reims in the Carolingian world of the latter ninth century,

> Hincmar, archbishop of Rheims (842-82) had made Rheims great.... He had made the preeminence of the see of the great Remigius a reality, had successfully exercised its metropolitical prerogatives, and had linked his authority with that of the west Frankish kings, particularly in the sphere of law and legislation, as well as providing crucial guidance to [the West Frankish kings] Charles the Bald, Louis the Stammerer, Carloman and his brother Louis III.[2]

As the *Annals* of Flodoard make evident, in the tenth century local interests were predominant in the life of the archdiocese, especially the attempt of

Count Heribert II of Vermandois to establish his power over the see.[3] Reims was worth the effort, for it was wealthy, possessed considerable landed estates, and could field military forces of considerable strength.[4]

The archbishops of Reims were not, however, entirely absent from the royal administration after Hincmar. Archbishop Heriveus (900-922) regained the office of archchancellor, the titular head of the royal writing office, supervising the royal notaries who drew up the king's documents, and held it from 910 until 919, as did his successors Artoldus (936-940) and Odalricus (949-961).[5] Nonetheless, in general, throughout the tenth century "Rheims strove to preserve its land from lay encroachment, to promote the religious life, to defend its wealth and its interests. National interests were subordinate…."[6] Despite its relative slide from political pre-eminence, Reims was still notable for the excellence of its library and archives, which had been assembled by Hincmar. In following years the production of manuscripts continued in its *scriptoria*, particularly those of St-Rémi and St-Thierry, and its cathedral school retained its high reputation.[7]

Reims had become a center of annalistic history when Fulk, the archchaplain to Louis the Pious, became administrator of the archdiocese and may have been involved in the writing of the *Annals of St-Bertin*, the continuation of the *Royal Frankish Annals*, which end in 829.[8] Archbishop Hincmar assumed the authorship of the *RFA* sometime after 860, and he continued working on them until his death in 882.[9] Thus Flodoard's *Annals* are a continuation of an already established tradition of the keeping of annals at Reims. This tradition was maintained almost into the eleventh century by Richer of Reims, whose *Historia* is also a continuation of the *Annals of St-Bertin* while making extensive use of Flodoard's *Annals* and *History of the Church of Reims*.

Flodoard of Reims

Flodoard is known to the modern world largely through writings that are not autobiographical. Nevertheless, we can be fairly certain that he was born in the 890s, either in 893 or 894, probably at Épernay, about 27 kilometers from Reims. As a youth, he was educated at the well-staffed cathedral school at Reims, which Archbishop Fulk (d. 900) had done much to develop. His career progressed at Reims rapidly. Following his schooling, which, along with a thorough grounding in the seven liberal arts, undoubtedly included a deep reading and respect for the work of Roman historians, he became a priest and canon of the cathedral of Reims and began directly to serve Archbishop Heriveus (d. 922) as what might well be considered the historian of the church of his diocese. Flodoard began this role in 919 (or perhaps a little earlier), when he commenced writing the *Annals*, a yearly account of current events often with a bias toward how these affected the interests of the archbishopric. In beginning the *Annals*, undoubtedly under the instructions of Archbishop Herveus, Flodoard played the key role in resuscitating a Reims tradition that Archbishop Hincmar (d. 882) had initiated when he undertook to continue the *Annals of St. Bertin* in 858.

Following Herveus's death, Flodoard was seconded to the staff of the new archbishop, Seulfus, with whom he already was well acquainted since the prelate previously had served as an archdeacon of Reims. Indeed, in 924, Flodoard indicates that he was serving in the archbishop's retinue when the latter accompanied King Raoul and Hugh of Provence to their important summit meeting with William of Aquitaine in the Autun region (6A-B of the *Annals*).[10] It seems likely that at this time Flodoard was already a canon of the Reims cathedral, as indicated by the benefices that he is known to have received.

The premature death of Archbishop Seulfus in 925 brought considerable uncertainty both to the archdiocese of Reims and to Flodoard's personal life. Count Heribert II of Vermandois was able to impose his son Hugh, not yet five years of age, as archbishop-elect of the cathedral of Reims (7G), although the diocese was actually managed by others on behalf of the child bishop (10B). Flodoard seems to have had no difficulty in accepting this arrangement, but because he had not participated in Hugh's election he was apparently considered to be recalcitrant by the men who now controlled the archiepiscopal administration in Hugh's name. Flodoard saw his benefices confiscated and may well have courted some personal danger (7G n.). However, when hostilities erupted between King Raoul and Hugh the Great of Paris on one side and Count Heribert II on the other in 931, Heribert lost Reims and the king imposed Hugh the Great's candidate, Artoldus, as archbishop of Reims, supplanting Heribert's son Hugh (13H). Again, Flodoard accepted the imposition of a new archiepiscopal regime.

Throughout these upheavals in the church of Reims, Flodoard continued his *Annals*. Despite his personal inclinations, Flodoard did not use his writing excessively to attack the prevailing political situation. Moreover, in order to maintain his obligations as historian of the church during this period, he would seem to have become something of an "ancient historian." It is to the 930s that scholars have generally assigned the writing of three important hagiographic works known collectively as *De triumphis Christi*, which probably were intended to be pieces of a great poetic epic: *De triumphis Christi sanctorumque Palestinae* ("On the Triumphs of Christ and the Saints of Palestine") in three books, *De triumphis Christi Antiochiae gestis* ("On the Triumphs of Christ Achieved at Antioch") in ten books, and *De Christi triumphis apud Italiam* ("On the Triumphs of Christ in Italy") in fourteen books. The works celebrate the achievements of men and women living in the world who nonetheless exhibited admirable saintliness and, thereby, brought about the triumph of Christ in the world. As the titles of the pieces indicate, each work was concerned with a different geographical region, and even in these metrical works Flodoard showed his historical inclination by presenting the saintly accomplishments of the saints in a chronological fashion.[11] These poetical works gained Flodoard considerable contemporary renown as an author and scholar but dealt with topics of no obvious contemporary political purpose. Indeed, it is likely that Flodoard's adversaries at Reims did not take the trouble to ferret out the occasional barbs directed against Count Heribert's vigorous intervention in archiepiscopal affairs.

In 936, Flodoard was sent to Rome, where he remained for about a year, likely over the conflict over the archiepiscopal see of Reims. However, this journey may also have served as a pilgrimage to the holy city for a cathedral canon seeking spiritual renewal in the wake of the difficulties at Reims. While in Rome, Flodoard likely was given an audience with Pope Leo VII and certainly was provided with hospitality (probably room and board) by the papal establishment. It is important to emphasize that during his stay at Rome, Flodoard continued his scholarly research and acquired considerable information for his as yet incomplete *De Christi triumphis apud Italiam.*

In 940, archbishops changed again when Count Heribert II, allied with William Longsword of Rouen, captured Reims, expelled Artoldus, and reinstalled his son Hugh as archbishop (22C). With this change of regime, however, Flodoard became personally involved when, as he was preparing to undertake a pilgrimage to the shrine of St. Martin at Tours, he was arrested by Count Heribert because of rumors that Flodoard opposed him and his son. Flodoard was held in detention for five months and suffered the loss of his holdings in the diocese of Reims (22F). Once the former archbishop Hugh had been restored to his see, he freed Flodoard from captivity (23D) and returned at least some of his former possessions.[12]

Although Pope Stephen IX acknowledged Hugh as the legitimate archbishop of Reims (24A-B), the murder of William Longsword and the death of Heribert II, both in 943 (25A), reopened the struggle for the domination of northeastern Francia,[13] which in 946 resulted in Reims being captured by King Louis IV and King Otto I of Germany. Archbishop Hugh was chased from the city and Artoldus, the former archbishop, was restored (28G), and again Flodoard accepted the new political and ecclesiastical reality.

After the reinstatement of Artoldus as archbishop, Flodoard was made the archivist of the cathedral of Reims. He served the archbishop closely, attending numerous synods and councils at such places as Verdun, Mouzon, Trier, and Ingelheim. In addition, Flodoard also carried out important diplomatic missions for Archbishop Artoldus and even served as an envoy of King Louis IV to Otto I. As though his diplomatic work and duties as archivist were not enough to keep him occupied, in the mid-950s Flodoard undertook to write a *History of the Church of Reims*. This work, which is heavily based upon the diplomatic sources, especially the letters of the archbishops preserved in the cathedral's archives, was an immense undertaking and remains a monument of medieval church history.[14] It covers the history of the church of Reims in four books, beginning with the foundation of the city itself and running until the end of the synods of Ingelheim and Trier, which resolved the dispute over the archbishopric of Reims between Artoldus and Hugh in 948 (30D-J, O-P).

Flodoard kept to his very busy schedule throughout his life. In 962, following the death of Archbishop Artoldus, he played a role as a canon of the cathedral church in the election of Odelricus to the archiepiscopal office (44H). However, in 963, Flodoard resigned his office as canon, which at this time he characterized as a "yoke," and arranged for his nephew, also named Flodoard, to be appointed in his place (45). Nevertheless, the elder Flodoard went on working in the archives and continued to write the *Annals*. In 966, these come to an abrupt end and in some of the manuscripts a necrology is appended to that year indicating that Flodoard had died in the spring at 73 years of age.

The *Annals*

Flodoard's *Annals* are an annual recording of current events. Flodoard strove to begin each year's events on 25 December, Christmas Day (the first day of the new year in the calendar used in northern Europe), and continues throughout the year to record the salient happenings of the period in close chronological order. Although he does not always succeed, his tendency to outline chains of events suggests that Flodoard had a certain interest in causation. In this way, it is likely that he was trying to show the way in which God worked through human agency to affect the world in which he lived. In the manner of his annalistic models, especially the *Annals of St. Bertin*, Flodoard often included in a year's entry noteworthy religious happenings, often miracles, in order to emphasize that the hand of God was always at work in human events. There were miraculous lightings of candles (2D, 6I), miraculous healings (4H, 6I, 13C, 14C, 16B), three people who came back from the dead (2D, 16E, 44E), religious visions (6I, 19D, 22G), and of course the inexplicable outbreak of fiery torments in people's bodies (27H), that is, St. Anthony's fire or ergotism as it is known today. In addition, he also recorded unusual natural phenomena such as lunar eclipses (8b, 18C), remarkable celestial displays (4F, 9A, 12C, 16E, 19C, 22E), strange weather such as especially severe storms (3F, 10B, 26G) and large hailstones (1), unusually harsh winters (46A), droughts (3F), and famines (24D).

Flodoard's broadly based system of values is clearly evident in his positive treatment of some protagonists in this ongoing story and his negative treatment of others. For example, he has nothing good to say of non-Christians. As a result, Vikings, Muslims, and Magyars are uniformly treated in a hostile manner but also often as a scourge sent by God to punish Christians who were not acting in an appropriate manner. It is less easy to find Flodoard's heroes, perhaps because he tends to follow the behavior of major figures in considerable detail and thus found them not to be consistently virtuous or in the right. Here the Aristotelian notion of the historian can be glimpsed or, to put it another way, as an historian Flodoard was not a poet who sought to provide the essence of the men and women about whom he wrote. Of particular importance in Flodoard's judgment was preserving the integrity and, indeed, the autonomy of the church of Reims. To put it simply, when anyone did wrong to Reims, the action was not defensible regardless of how positively the person may have acted on other occasions. In short, the church was good even if some of the people connected with it might not always be good.

The church of Reims was at the center of many major political interactions at the highest level of society throughout Flodoard's life as historian and archivist. In addition, as noted above, Flodoard was very close to a series of archbishops over the course of four decades and worked as a diplomat in the service of his church and of the west Frankish king. As a result, Flodoard was positioned to be exceptionally well informed regarding important events throughout the northern half of Francia (Neustria and Austrasia), and also in Lotharingia, the northern half of the former *Francia Media*. His information, therefore, is most complete for this broad northern region. Nevertheless, he also provides information regarding events both in the southern reaches of the *regnum Francorum* (Aquitaine and Burgundy) and in the so-called Lombard *regnum* of northern Italy and the papacy.

Political intrigue is high on the list of subjects that interested Flodoard and he provides a surprising level of detail regarding matters such as secret negotiations, duplicitous treaties, and unsuccessful plots. The reader is often left wondering how he obtained such information as he rarely divulges his sources. However, if Flodoard were merely reconstructing what happened behind the scenes on the basis of fragments of information that subsequently became available or how events played out, he demonstrates a detective's sense for the reconstruction of human interactions on the political level. However, it also is likely that his extensive familiarity with the classical tradition of history writing as represented, for example, by the works of Livy and Sallust, and of poetry, exemplified by his deep understanding of both Vergil and Lucan, cannot have been a hindrance. In short, a combination of his personal acquaintance with many of the major protagonists (both in terms of understanding their motivations and their ability to divulge information), the "paper trail" that crossed his desk as archivist, and his grasp of the way in which Roman historians understood political behavior may all have played a role in his writing. Flodoard very likely never read Tacitus but he would seem to have followed many of the same methods.

Flodoard tends to be a sound and straightforward guide to the *realia* of the world of which he writes. For example, he provides the details of military organization without either epic intonation or romantic flourishes. Indeed, even the *rustici*, who often get short shrift in historical works written for aristocratic patrons, are seen to play their role in the system of local defense. Expeditionary levies are shown operating outside of their home districts both in the field and in siege operations. The *obsequia* or military households of the magnates, both lay and ecclesiastical, are clearly the standing armies of the time but they have no natural propensity to win against all odds in struggles with men of lesser status in society. Warfare is shown to be brutal and duplicitous. There is no hint of the "chivalry" and "Romance" that some modern writers want to impose on later medieval martial behavior.

Flodoard's *Annals* may well be considered a useful example of the work of a medieval author who strove to get the facts right for his readers. In short, modern scholars regard him as consistently providing accurate information concerning political and ecclesiastical matters. This would appear to be the case, it is claimed, despite Flodoard's clear personal bias in favor of vindicating the rights of the church of Reims. It may perhaps be argued that he omitted facts from the *Annals* of which he was aware when he wrote and thus through these omissions provided a biased view of a particular situation. However, any such allegations must be proven and not simply asserted as though the omission of any fact is in itself a distortion. Obviously, one cannot write everything one knows. A substantive distortion of fact must be caused by the omission, and for the author to be deemed dishonest there must be an intent to distort.

The Political Background to the *Annals*

The emperor Charlemagne (d. 814), the great Frankish ruler, controlled a vast collection of lands that he had inherited as well as conquered. His empire included almost all of modern France and stretched south over the Pyrenees to incorporate the Spanish March centered on Barcelona, Germany to the Elbe and Danube, and northern and central Italy. These lands, the various *regna* under his power, and the imperial title passed to his one surviving legitimate son, Louis the Pious. However, when the latter died in 840, the empire was divided into three parts among his surviving sons and in subsequent decades further divisions were made. Louis's three surviving sons divided the empire into three independent kingdoms. The West Frankish Kingdom (*Francia Occidentalis*), which became the basis upon which the medieval French kingdom was built, went to Charles the Bald. Louis the German received the East Frankish Kingdom (*Francia Orientalis*), which was to serve as the basis for the development of the kingdom of Germany. Lothair, the eldest, received the imperial title and *Francia Media*, that is, the Middle Kingdom that stretched from the Netherlands in the north to Rome in the south.

The Middle Kingdom (*Francia Media*)

In the years that followed the death of Louis's sons, the Carolingian kingdoms were divided and redivided with great frequency. When Lothair I, king of *Francia Media*, died in 855, his lands were divided among his three sons. Italy and the imperial title went to the eldest, Louis (Emperor Louis II). The northern part from Frisia through Alsace and Lorraine was inherited by Lothair II and came to be called Lotharingia (Lorraine in French, Lothair's Kingdom, *regnum Lotharii*, in Flodoard's general usage). A third or southwestern kingdom was also created. This *regnum*, called the Kingdom of Provence, was given to Charles and was composed largely of the Burgundian region. Charles's death without heirs in 863 was followed by the division of his kingdom between his two brothers. Lothair II died in 869 without legitimate heirs and his two uncles, Charles the Bald and Louis the German, divided his kingdom between them.

The West Frankish Kingdom (*Francia Occidentalis*)

Charles the Bald was succeeded in 877 by his only surviving son, Louis II the Stammerer, who inherited all of *Francia Occidentalis*. However, Louis died only sixteen months later and his inheritance was divided between his two sons, Louis III and Carloman, by his first marriage. Louis received the northern part of the kingdom (Neustria and Francia), and Carloman the southern half (Aquitaine and Burgundy). However, Charles the Bald's brother-in-law, Boso, who was one of the great magnates of *Francia Occidentalis* and held extensive lands and offices in both Provence and Burgundy, refused to recognize this division and proclaimed himself king. With the deaths of Louis III (882) and Carloman (884), Boso maintained his usurpation until his own death in 887. At that point the magnates of *Francia Occidentalis* chose Charles the Fat, king of *Francia Orientalis*, as their ruler and for the first time since 840, all of the *regnum Francorum* was theoretically united (see below).

The East Frankish Kingdom (*Francia Orientalis*)

When Louis the German died in 876, his three sons became independent kings over the territories they already ruled under their father. Carloman held Bavaria, Louis the Younger held the northern region of Saxony, and Charles the Fat had Swabia in the southwest. However, further devolution to an increasing multiplicity of *regna* in Germany was thwarted by the premature death of Carloman (880) and of Louis the Younger (882), both of whom died without leaving legitimate heirs. Thus, the surviving brother Charles the Fat inherited the entirety of *Francia Orientalis* that his father had ruled. Moreover, in 880, Charles the Fat succeeded in gaining recognition as king of Carolingian Italy and was awarded the imperial title. As noted above, he became king of *Francia Occidentalis* and thus officially united the empire that his grandfather, Louis the Pious, received from Charlemagne in 814. Charles, however, was opposed in Germany by his nephew, Arnulf of Carinthia, an illegitimate son of Carloman, and late in 887 was ousted from power. The story that he was too fat to carry out his duties, which included the defense of his realm, is doubtless apocryphal.

The Second Fragmentation of the Carolingian Empire

Following the fall of Charles the Fat, Arnulf ruled in the eastern kingdom. In the western kingdom, the nobles were unwilling to accept Charles the Simple, the son of Louis II, now aged nine, as their king. Instead, they turned to Count Odo of Paris (son of Robert the Strong, named *marchio* of Neustria by Charles the Bald specifically to combat the attacks of the Northmen), who had gained renown for himself by defending Paris from the Vikings. Louis (later to be called "the Blind"), the son of Boso and a grandson of Emperor Louis II of Italy, had been adopted[15] by Charles the Fat and, although only ten years of age, was chosen by the magnates to rule in Provence. However, in the region of Upper Burgundy to the east of the Jura, between the river Saône and the Alps, Count Rudolf (nephew of Judith, second wife of Louis the Pious) was proclaimed king. Flodoard calls this the kingdom of Cisalpine Gaul. Aquitaine, which had frequently been ruled by its own king under the early Carolingians, saw Count Ramnulf of Poitou raised to royal estate, but he died in 890 and the office with him. Finally, Guy II, count of Spoleto, emerged as the king of Carolingian Italy and was crowned emperor by Pope Stephen V in 891. These six kingdoms—the West Frankish kingdom, Lotharingia, the East Frankish kingdom, Provence, Upper Burgundy, and Italy—had a lasting presence after 888 and set the backdrop on a royal scale for the action described by Flodoard in his *Annals*.

The Events in Flodoard's *Annals*

Royal Affairs

Following the death of Odo in 898, Charles the Simple was finally raised to the kingship by the magnates of *Francia Occidentalis* (898-922). Indeed, Flodoard begins his *Annals* in 919 just as strong opposition was rising against King Charles. The ostensible reason for this opposition was Charles's putative favoritism toward certain Lotharingians (the magnates of Lotharingia had accepted Charles as their king in 911 on the death of the East Frankish king Louis the Child) to whom he is said to have granted various lands and offices in the western kingdom. This criticism focused on one particular favorite, Count Hagano, who had been related to Charles's deceased Lotharingian wife Frederuna (d. 917). The opposition to Charles was led by the brother of the deceased King Odo, Count Robert of Paris, and his son Hugh, later to be called the Great. Count Robert dominated virtually all of Neustria (the region between the Seine and the Loire) and was supported by Count Heribert II of Vermandois. Count Heribert's wife Adele was the daughter of Count Robert and the latter was married to Heribert's sister Beatrice. Heribert, a descendant of Charlemagne in the male line through King Bernard of Italy (see genealogical chart 1), was avidly pursuing a policy of territorial expansion in the area north of Reims. Another ally of Count Robert was his son-in-law Raoul, duke of Burgundy. The latter's father, Richard "the Justiciar," whom he succeeded in 921, created the duchy of Burgundy (not to be confused with the Transjurane Kingdom of Burgundy of Rudolf I).

In 922, while King Charles was in Lotharingia, Count Robert rebelled and claimed the throne, and the Frankish magnates living west of the Meuse transferred their allegiance to the usurper, who was crowned king at Reims (4E). Charles returned and moved against Robert but was defeated in battle (June 923). However, Robert was killed in the fighting and his son-in-law Raoul of Burgundy succeeded to the leadership of his side and was crowned king. Meanwhile King Charles was captured by Heribert II of Vermandois (5G). As king (923-36), Raoul, whose base was in the southeast, relied heavily on his brothers-in-law, Hugh the Great and Heribert of Vermandois, to sustain his rule in the north. As a result, Heribert gained possession of the important city and bishopric of Reims (5M), but to his chagrin he was not permitted also to take control of the old Carolingian capital at Laon (9A), which the king wanted to maintain as his own base in the north (10A, 13H, 17A). As a result, Heribert and Raoul were at odds and the latter relied heavily on his wife Queen Emma, a sister of Hugh the Great, to lead the royal party in Francia when the king was in Burgundy.

Raoul worked vigorously to protect and extend royal power in the north. For example, he developed productive relations with the Northmen who had been established at Rouen since 911. When William Longsword, the ruler of the Northmen, recognized Raoul's rule in 933, the king gave him additional lands (15B). For a time, Raoul attempted to gain acceptance as king in Lotharingia (5I, J, 6E), which had remained loyal to Charles the Simple, but by 925 King Henry I of Germany had succeeded in taking over the entire region (7G, and see below). Raoul was also active in the south. He was successful in gaining recognition from William II, count of Poitou, and other leading men of Aquitaine. Moreover, he carried out victorious campaigns against the Northmen who had invaded Burgundy and Aquitaine (7A, 12A, 17B).

Count Heribert II of Vermandois, whose control of Reims made him important to Flodoard, dominates events in the *Annals* until his death in 943. His efforts to take control of the fortress city of Laon and its region for his son Odo following the death of Count Roger in 926 were thwarted by King Raoul. As a result, Heribert attempted to restore Charles the Simple, who had been his captive for seven years, to the kingship. In these maneuvers, Heribert looked to the east for allies. He relied strongly on the support of his son-in-law Count Arnulf of Flanders, developed a working arrangement with Duke Gislebert of Lotharingia, and established an alliance with King Henry I of Germany. As a result of these policies, Heribert and Hugh the Great broke relations in 931, and thus Hugh and King Raoul were usually at war with the count of Vermandois.

This alliance succeeded in blunting Heribert's power and, following the death of King Raoul and King Henry in 936, Hugh the Great, son of King Robert I, emerged as the leading figure in Francia. He took the initiative and, acting as the kingmaker, summoned from exile in England Louis, son of Charles the Simple and thus his own nephew.[16] Hugh arranged for the installation of the youth as King Louis IV (936-54) (18A). The latter has been given the sobriquet *d'Outre-Mer* ("from overseas") by French historians.

In 937, Louis IV tried to assert his independence from Hugh the Great. As a result, Hugh strengthened his own position by resuscitating his alliance with Heribert II of Vermandois and soon after he married Hadwig, the sister of King Otto I of Germany. This set the stage for a new cycle of war in Francia. Louis IV developed an alliance with Duke Gislebert, who hoped to reassert Lotharingian independence from the German king, and captured the Carolingian royal city of Laon (20B). In addition, Louis made an alliance with Hugh the Black (20B, 21A), the brother of King Raoul and his successor in Burgundy, whose position was threatened by Hugh the Great and Heribert. In this struggle for power, William Longsword, who ruled the Northmen in the region that was to become Normandy, held the balance of power. However, after Louis IV and Hugh the Black of Burgundy successfully campaigned against him, William realized that maintaining a posture of independence was unproductive and allied himself with the royal party. However, Louis's eastern policy in support of Lotharingian independence from Otto I was crushed in battle by the latter. Thus, when Duke Gislebert of Lotharingia died, Louis IV pursued a new eastern policy. He married Gislebert's widow Gerberga (21G), a sister of King Otto. As a result, Otto, who was the most powerful ruler in Europe, became the arbiter of events in Francia through the marriage of his two sisters to Hugh and Louis.

The vexing problem of who would be the archbishop of Reims was re-kindled in 940 when William Longsword abandoned his alliance with Louis, joined with Hugh the Great and Heribert II, and captured the city. In the wake of this victory, the allies expelled Archbishop Artoldus, the king's archchancellor, and reinstalled Heribert's son Hugh to his former position as archbishop of Reims (22C). This highly uncanonical act was legitimized by an episcopal synod (23D) and subsequently recognized by Pope Stephen IX, who sent the *pallium*[17] to Hugh (24B).

However, the political scene changed dramatically in 942. Willliam Longsword was murdered by agents of the count of Flanders (25A, and see below), who was a close ally of Heribert. This destroyed the Paris-Verman-dois-Rouen alliance and enabled King Louis to appear as the protector of William's son, Richard I, while himself gaining considerable influence over affairs at Rouen (25A, 25B, and see below). The anti-royal party was further weakened the next year when Heribert II of Vermandois died leaving behind a brood of quarrelsome sons who found it necessary to come to terms with the king (25C). Hugh the Great, seeing his allies either dead, hostile, or in dis-array, came to terms with Louis IV. As a sign of his loyalty, Hugh stood as bap-tismal sponsor for Louis's daughter and was established by the king as *dux* of Francia (*dux Francorum*) (25E), which signified that Hugh was the virtual viceroy of the kingdom.

By 944, however, the two men were again in conflict as each had designs upon dominating the Rouen polity. In this struggle, Louis was captured by the Northman Harold, who was holding Bayeux (27E), and in a complicated matrix of machinations ostensibly was handed over as a prisoner to Hugh the Great (27G). In what amounted to a ransom, Louis obtained his freedom by surrendering the fortress of Laon to Hugh who then once again recognized his former prisoner as his king (28E). But Hugh had been shortsighted. Gerberga arranged for her brother Otto I to support Louis, and although the German army failed to take Laon, it did capture Reims in 946. Archbishop Hugh was forced to flee (27G) and Louis reversed the decision of 940 by restoring Artoldus as archbishop. Several church synods not only affirmed

Artoldus's reinstatement but also excommunicated Hugh the Great (29H, J, 30A, D, O). Finally, the case was sent to the pope at Rome, who confirmed Artoldus in possession of the archbishopric. In the frequent conflicts between Louis and Hugh, Otto I usually supported the former and thus the royal power in Francia was maintained (30K, 32A).

Louis IV's son Lothair (954-86) was only thirteen years of age when his father died. As a result, the queen mother Gerberga was most anxious for a rapprochement with her brother-in-law Hugh the Great, who once again was the most powerful figure in Francia (36C). In return for supporting Lothair's accession to the throne, Hugh was given power to rule as sort of a viceroy in both Aquitaine and Burgundy (36F). Most of Aquitaine eluded effective control from the north, but when he died in 956 (38D), Hugh the Great was able to pass on the duchy of Burgundy to his son Odo while another of his sons Hugh (later called Capet), who was to become king in Francia in 987, succeeded in Paris as *dux Francorum* (42B).

Queen Gerberga was fortunate in having another powerful supporter in her brother Bruno, archbishop of Cologne and administrator of Lotharingia for his brother Otto I of Germany (35F, and see below). The archbishop, presumably in accord with Otto's policy, provided consistent support for Gerberga and the young King Lothair (38D, 40B, 41D, 42B, 44A). However, he was also protective of his sister Hadwig, widow of Hugh the Great, and her sons (40B, 41A, 42B). Certainly, Lothair had a more successful reign than his father. This may been been due in part to the death of Hugh the Great and the division of his lands among his young sons, the death of Heribert II of Vermandois with the division of his lands, and the death of Count Arnulf of Flanders (47B). However, on the whole the hand of the German king manifested through the efforts of his brother, Archbishop Bruno, may be seen with some irony as the major determinant in this last success of the Carolingian dynasty.

The matter of the archbishopric of Reims again arose to disrupt the kingdom when Archbishop Artoldus died in 961 and Hugh Capet led an effort to restore the diocese to the ousted former archbishop Hugh, his own cousin (43B). However, Bruno opposed this, as did King Lothair's other uncle, Bishop Rorico of Laon.[18] The matter was left to the adjudication of Pope John XII, who decided against the claims of the former archbishop Hugh (44H), and a certain Odelricus, known more for his piety than his political connections, was ordained archbishop of Reims (44H). The pope's decision in favor of Archbishop Bruno's policy likely was motivated by the fact that Otto I, who had been king of Italy since 952, acquired the imperial title in 962 and controlled Rome (44B, and see below).

Northern Powers: Flanders and the Northmen

As the above brief account of politics indicates, the counts of Flanders and the rulers of Rouen were two of the most important powers in the northern parts of the West Frankish kingdom. The county of Flanders began to take shape during the later ninth century under Baldwin I, "Iron Arm" (d. 879). In 860, he married Judith, a daughter of King Charles the Bald. The latter subsequently established his son-in-law in what contemporaries call the *pagus Flandrensis.* His son, Baldwin II (879–918), expanded the territory under comital control and was deeply involved in the political maneuverings of the West Frankish kingdom after the death of Charles the Fat. Baldwin II generally opposed the Robertian king Odo and supported the Carolingians, first Arnulf of Carinthia, then Charles the Simple, and finally Arnulf's son Zwentibold. Baldwin also favored the tactic of assassinating his enemies and opponents, arranging the murders of both Fulk, archbishop of Reims, and Heribert I of Vermandois. Baldwin was allied to the Anglo-Saxon kings of England through his marriage to Aelfthryth, daughter of King Alfred the Great. Thus Baldwin's son and successor Arnulf I "the Great" (918–65), who figures prominently throughout the entire *Annals* of Flodoard, was a descendant of both Charlemagne through his grandmother Judith and of Alfred the Great through his mother.

Arnulf I continued his father's policy of territorial expansion to the south, aiming especially at the county of Artois, whose control was dependent on possession of the fortress of Montreuil-sur-Mer in the county of Ponthieu. Arnulf's southward expansion naturally clashed with the interests of the counts of Ponthieu as well as with the policies of the Northmen of Rouen (see below) who sought territorial aggrandizement to the north and east. Arnulf generally could rely on the support of Heribert II of Vermandois, whose daughter Adele married Arnulf in 934 (16D). Much of the conflict reported in the *Annals* focuses on the conflict between Arnulf and the Northmen of Rouen. This conflict is symbolized by Flodoard in his account of the struggle for control of the stronghold of Montreuil-sur-Mer, which is depicted as being defended stoutly by the counts of Ponthieu, Erluinus and his son Roger. Arnulf, following what would seem to have become a traditional Flemish tactic, orchestrated the assassination of William Longsword in 942 (25A) and thus thoroughly destabilized the balance of power.

Also figuring prominently in Flodoard's *Annals* are the Northmen, the last representatives of the Viking raiders who greatly affected life in the West Frankish kingdom throughout the ninth century. While it is common for modern scholars to focus on Northmen under the leadership of Rollo, who had been given lands around Rouen by Charles the Simple in 911 (see above), Flodoard makes it clear that many other groups of Northmen were in the field as well. He gives particular attention to those operating on the river Loire under the leadership of Ragenold who were regarded as a menace, especially to Brittany. They are reported to have been responsible for considerable material destruction and particularly for the capture of significant numbers of people (1) who were transported to Scandinavia as slaves while others fled to England. Flodoard records that Count Robert of Paris conceded Brittany and its major port city of Nantes to the Loire Vikings (3G). He emphasizes that both Hugh the Great and Heribert II of Vermandois reconfirmed this concession (9B). Ragenold was involved also in the wider politics of Francia, conducting operations in conjunction with the Northmen at Rouen in support of King Charles the Simple (5H). However, Ragenold's effort to obtain a degree of territorial control in Burgundy was repulsed (7A) and a later invasion by the Loire Northmen into Aquitaine was a disastrous failure (12A, 17D). Bretons living under Norse rule rebelled (13G) but were defeated by Ragenold's successor Incon (13H). However, with the return of exiles from England and the aid of the Anglo-Saxon king, Bretons were able to regain much of their land from the Northmen (19E, 21G).

Despite the number of Norse groups and their diverse impacts, it has become all too easy, with the benefit of hindsight, to focus on the Northmen of Rouen under Rollo as the founders of Normandy. However, Flodoard himself gives no indication that Rollo and his successors were superior to or more legitimate than the Northmen on the Loire. Flodoard refers to Rollo and his son William Longsword as *principes* (7E, 15B), but he does the same with regard to Ragenold (5H). He refers to Felecan, a commander of Loire Northmen who invaded Brittany, as *dux* (13G), which seems to have its original Latin meaning of a general or military commander, but it is also the same word that is translated as "duke" and commonly applied in modern histories to Rollo and his successors at Rouen. In short, the political dynamic by which Rollo's successors came to be the most successful of the Northmen in the long term can be glimpsed from Flodoard's account but, while telling the story, he could not see the ultimate result of which his modern readers are aware.

Rollo appears infrequently in the *Annals*, fighting against King Raoul over the fortress of Eu (7E) and supporting Charles the Simple against Heribert II of Vermandois (9C, 10A). His son William Longsword (930-42) was much more deeply involved in the general affairs of the West Frankish kingdom. He gained additional lands from King Raoul in 933 (15B), opposed the movement of Count Arnulf of Flanders to the south (21A and see above), and was a consistent ally of his father-in-law, Heribert II of Vermandois. When Count Arnulf arranged the assassination of William Longsword at the end of 942, King Louis IV supported the succession of William's son Richard I (942-96), but Richard's position was not secured until after several years of disorder in the territory of Rouen. There was a pagan revival as well as the arrival of Northmen from the larger Scandinavian world, but King Louis IV and his allies, Arnulf of Flanders and Heribert of Vermandois, were able to defeat both of these threats (25B, 26I). Louis IV then attempted to use his domination of Rouen to augment his power but was captured by Harold, the Northman in command of Bayeux (27E). By the end of the 940s the Northmen of Rouen were associated with Hugh the Great and participated in military campaigns with him (30N, 31E). As Richard I came of age, he also allied with the family of Hugh the Great by marrying Hugh's daughter Emma in 960 (42B).

Southern Powers: Aquitaine and the Duchy of Burgundy

In the southern portion of *Francia Occidentalis*, the duchy and sometime kingdom of Aquitaine had a lengthy and complex history before the division of the Carolingian empire by the Treaty of Verdun in 843. However, the duchy as it appears in the *Annals* seems to have begun to take form during the reign of King Odo (888-98). After the death of Count Ramnulf II of Poitou, his young son and heir Ebalus was opposed by the eastern Aquitanian magnate William the Pious, count of the Auvergne and of Gothia (889-918), who took the title *dux Aquitanorum* (duke of the Aquitainians) in 898. William the Pious died in 918 and was succeeded by his nephew William II (918-26). Thus, while the Aquitainians acknowledged Charles the Simple as king in 898, they were reluctant to support the non-Carolingian kings Robert I and Raoul. King Raoul, as seen above, obtained recognition from Duke William II by returning Berry to him in 924 (6A). Other southern nobles gave their support to Raoul more slowly, but eventually Raymond-Pons III, count of Toulouse, Ermengaudus, count of Rouergue (14D), and Charles Constantine, count of Vienne (13A), acknowledged him as king.

   After his accession in 936, King Louis IV also desired to have his position accepted south of the Loire and made repeated journeys there (22E, 23F, 26A, 33A) to receive the acknowledgments of William Towhead, count of Poitou (who succeeded William II as count of the Auvergne), Raymond-Pons III of Toulouse, and other powerful men of the region. Upon Louis's death in 954, Hugh the Great enlisted the young king Lothair in his futile attempt to extend his domination over Aquitaine (37B).

   When he became king of the West Franks in 923, Raoul retained the duchy of Burgundy as his base of power. When he died without a direct male heir in 936, his brother Hugh the Black succeeded him as *dux*, but only after a struggle against Hugh the Great (18B, 18D). As has been seen, Hugh the Black was a supporter of King Louis IV (20B) in the struggles of the king against Hugh the Great and Heribert II of Vermandois. When Hugh the Black died in 952,

Hugh the Great, with the support of King Lothair, succeeded in taking control of the Burgundian duchy (36F). Following Hugh's death in 956, Burgundy was given first to his son Odo (42B) and then, after Odo's death, to Odo's brother Otto-Henry (see 47A and note).

Lotharingia and Germany

The history of Lotharingia figures prominently in the *Annals* of Flodoard because its western frontier on the river Meuse was a mere 80 kilometers from the city of Reims. Moreover, the eastern regions of the diocese of Reims were in Lotharingia proper, as was the diocese of Cambrai, which belonged in the ecclesiastical province of the archbishopric. However, the fate of Lotharingia was also connected intimately to Germany, the kingdom of the East Franks. Lotharingia ceased to have its own king when Zwentibold was defeated and killed in 900. Thus Louis the Child, the king of the East Franks, absorbed the region into his *regnum* and established Gebhard as *dux* to administer this district on the frontiers with the West Frankish kingdom. Following the death of Louis the Child in 911, the Lotharingians accepted the Carolingian Charles the Simple, the West Frankish king, as their ruler because the East Frankish magnates had elected the non-Carolingian Duke Conrad of Franconia as their king. The overthrow of Charles the Simple in the West was in part an anti-Lotharingian reaction and, as a result, many of the Lotharingians refused to acknowledge Raoul as their king.

With the death of King Conrad in 918, the German kingdom saw a smooth transition to the rule of Duke Henry of Saxony, known as "the Fowler" (919-36). Interestingly, Flodoard styles Henry simply as *princeps* and not as king (*rex*) up to 923 (5A), which may well cast some doubt upon the legitimacy of this non-Carolingian in the eyes of an observer in Reims. King Henry took advantage of the discord in the western kingdom to expand his power over Lotharingia. Flodoard records the pacts made between Henry I and Charles the Simple (3E, 3I), as well as the one that Henry made with Count Robert of Paris (5A). By 925 Henry had conquered Lotharingia (5L, 7D, 8E). Count Gislebert, whom Flodoard depicts as the leader of the Lotharingians (2C), was endowed by Henry with ducal powers and married Henry's daughter Gerberga (later the wife of King Louis IV).

Germany suffered severely from Magyar raids during the weak reign of Conrad and the noble leaders of the various regions of the realm gained considerable independence. Henry I, by contrast, rebuilt the basis for royal power in the eastern kingdom with his successful defense against the Magyars, which was highlighted by his victory at Riade in 933 (15A). Henry I was succeeded by his son Otto I (936-73) and Flodoard records most of the important events of Otto's reign. Flodoard also describes support for the succession of Otto's younger brother Henry in 936 (18B), and he knew of the German king's expeditions to Italy, his marriage to Adelaid in 951 (33H), and the family conflict sparked by that marriage (35B, 35E, 36D). Flodoard also chronicles Otto's great victory over the Magyars at the battle of the Lechfeld in 955 (37A) and his coronation as emperor at Rome in 962 (44B).

Otto's disputed succession in 936 tempted some Lotharingians, led by Duke Gislebert, to switch their loyalties to the Carolingian Louis IV, who had just been installed as king of the West Franks following the death of King Raoul (21B, 21C, and see above). After initial hesitation, the new western king made a determined effort to reimpose West Frankish rule on Lotharingia, but Otto's military success and Gislebert's death in 939 (21F) put an end to Louis IV's martial efforts to the east. However, as seen above, Louis IV altered his policy radically when he married Gislebert's widow Gerberga, Otto's sister, with the German king's blessing (21B-D, G). With friendly relations established, Otto established himself as the arbiter in the conflict between Louis IV and his other brother-in-law, Hugh the Great of Paris. Otto I generally supported the West Frankish king and thus propped up the Carolingian monarchy. In this way, his nephew Lothair ultimately would rule *Francia Occidentalis*.

Following the failed rebellion in Lotharingia, Otto I established his brother Henry to replace Gislebert (22E). Henry, however, was involved in a plot to kill Otto (unrecorded by Flodoard) and the German king named Count Otho of Verdun as *dux* (24C). By 945, following Otho's death, the *dux* of Lotharingia was Conrad the Red (27G), a descendant of Gebhard, King Louis the Child's nominee as *dux* a generation earlier. Conrad then was associated with the royal family by marrying King Otto's daughter Liutgard. However, in 953 Duke Conrad played a leading role in the revolt by Liudolf, King Otto's son, and was removed from office (35B). Conrad did not accept this initial defeat and allied with the Magyars, whom he induced to invade Lotharingia (36A). However, in 955, he finally made his peace with Otto (37C) and met a meritorious death in the great victory of the German king at the Lechfeld in the same year (37C). Conrad had been replaced as *dux* in Lotharingia by Archbishop Bruno of Cologne, King Otto's brother (39B). The latter consistently acted as mediator if not arbiter of affairs in the West Frankish kingdom between the party of his sister Gerberga, widow of King Louis IV (d. 954), and that of his sister Hadwig, the widow of Hugh the Great.

Upper Burgundy, Provence, and Italy

Three additional kingdoms figure prominently in Flodoard's *Annals*. The kingdom of Transjurane (Upper) Burgundy, Cisalpine Gaul in Flodoard's terms, was in the hands of the descendants of its founder Rudolf I (888-912). Rudolf II (912-37) failed in his attempt to become king of Italy after the overthrow of King Berengar in 922 (4B, 6D), but he remained secure in his rule of Burgundy. In 935, Rudolph established friendly relations with King Raoul of the West Franks and King Henry I of the East Franks (17A). In 937 Rudolf II was succeeded by his young son Conrad the Peaceful (19E), who was essentially a captive of King Otto I of Germany (22E), and he remained under Otto's tutelage until reaching the age of majority.

The history of the kingdom of Burgundy was closely intertwined with that of the kingdom of Provence. After the blinding of King Louis in 905, the Provençal kingdom was effectively administered by Louis's cousin, Count Hugh of Arles (himself a descendant of Emperor Lothair, son of Louis the Pious, 8D n.). Like Rudolf II of Burgundy, Hugh ventured into Italian affairs but by contrast succeeded in gaining recognition as king of Italy in 926 (8D). Now a king in his own right, Hugh demonstrated a much reduced interest in Provence and ceded the region of Vienne to Heribert II of Vermandois (10D), and in 933 he handed over to King Rudolf II of Burgundy all of his own lands in Provence in return for Rudolf's promise to stay out of Italy (19E n.).

Affairs at Rome, as seen above, were of interest not only to the kings and dukes in the south but also to Otto I. Flodoard was well informed on events in Rome because a constant stream of pilgrims and envoys going there from Francia passed through Reims on their return. For example, he reported the capture of Pope John X by the brother of King Hugh of Italy, the *marchio* Guy of Tuscany (10B) and he knew details of the rebellion in Rome against King Hugh led by Hugh's stepson Alberic II of Spoleto (15A).

When Rudolf II of Burgundy died (937), King Hugh of Italy positioned himself to claim that kingdom. He married Rudolf's widow Bertha and arranged for his own son Lothair to marry the deceased king's daughter Adelaid.[19] However, King Otto I intervened vigorously in this scheme and secured the succession in Burgundy of Rudolf II's son Conrad the Peaceful, whom he sequestered at the German court. In Italy, opposition to King Hugh's rule was led by Count Berengar of Ivrea, and in 945 the monarch agreed to abdicate in order to assure by treaty the succession of his son Lothair to the Italian throne. Hugh then returned to Provence where he died in 947.

Lothair was king in Italy in name only, for Berengar of Ivrea was the true power behind the throne.[20] In 950 Lothair died, by poisoning according to rumors known to Flodoard (32F), and Berengar was chosen king and associated his son Adalbert in the office (32F and n.). However, Lothair's widow Adelaid presented some attractive options to political opportunists who had designs on the Italian throne. As the daughter of King Rudolf II, sister of King Conrad the Peaceful, and widow of King Lothair, she represented plausible claims to the kingdom of Burgundy as well as to the kingdom of Italy. King Berengar imprisoned her to remove her from the political scene but Adelaid appealed to Otto I, protector of her brother Conrad, for help. In 951, Otto I invaded Italy and first liberated and then married Adelaid (33H). Otto was able to gain general recognition as king in Italy and eventually Berengar accepted the superior position of Otto (34B), although the peace between them was uneasy. Berengar renewed hostilities against German interests, which played a role in encouraging Otto to make another expedition to Italy in 962, and at this time Otto had himself crowned emperor in Rome by Pope John XII (44B).

England

England appears peripherally but significantly in the *Annals*. King Charles the Simple was married to Eadgifu, a daughter of the Anglo-Saxon ruler King Edward the Elder (899-925), and Hugh the Great, the son of Charles's great rival Count Robert of Paris, took as his second wife Eadhild, another daughter of Edward the Elder (8E). To round out the family connections, Edith, a third daughter of King Edward, was married to Otto I, king of Germany. When Charles the Simple was captured by Heribert II of Vermandois (5G), Eadgifu and her son Louis took refuge at the court of her father Edward the Elder and of her brother King Aethelstan (925-39). On the death of King Raoul, Hugh the Great arranged the repatriation of his wife's nephew Louis IV from England (18A), and King Aethelstan provided naval support, futile as it turned out, in Louis's attempt to regain Lotharingia (21D). When Louis IV was taken captive by Hugh the Great, King Edmund, Louis's uncle and former brother-in-law of Hugh, worked to gain the king's release from captivity (28C). Flodoard was also aware of the support that King Aethelstan gave to Breton exiles in England when they attempted to regain their land from the Northmen who had seized it (18A).

The Magyars

The rivals for power within the various regions of the kingdoms that emerged from the Carolingian Empire created substantial internal disorder. However, this was exacerbated by the arrival of the Magyars (the ancestors of the Hungarians, consistently called *Hungari* by Flodoard) into the area of the

Carpathian basin at the end of the ninth century. The Magyars were a nomadic people speaking a Finno-Ugric language who previously dwelled in the region to the northeast of the Black Sea. They had been involved in Byzantine politics, especially in fighting against their neighbors, the Pechenegs, and had even been enlisted as mercenaries by King Arnulf of Germany in 892. However, by 896 they had been defeated by the Bulgars and began their movement to the west. Once settled in what would become Hungary, the Magyars carried out wide-ranging raids throughout western Europe as far as Spain, often in cooperation with one or another western leader who used them as mercenaries (4B, 36A).

Flodoard records raids by the Magyars on Italy and Lotharingia in 919 (1), on Italy as they assisted the deposed King Berengar in 922 and 924 (4B, 6D), and into Francia in 926, 937, 951, and 954 (8B, 8C, 19C, 19D, 33E, 36A). He also reports successful defenses against the Magyars, the victory of King Henry I of Germany at the battle of Riade in 933 (15A), King Raoul's operations that forced them out of Burgundy in 935 (17B), and King Otto I's victories in 954 (36A) and especially in the renowned battle of the Lechfeld in 955 (37C), which put an end to Magyar offensive aspirations in the west. Flodoard knew the Magyars to be pagans (19C, D), but after their defeat in 955 Christianity was spread more widely among them by western missionaries. The coronation of King Stephen in the year 1000 with the approbation of both the pope and King Otto III of Germany established the status of the kingdom of the Magyars as one of the Christian states of the west.

The Saracens

The Saracens, or more accurately Muslims, although of much less consequence to the west than the Magyars, nevertheless appear frequently in Flodoard's *Annals*. Muslim raids against various parts of Italy and settlements throughout the peninsula had been common throughout the middle third of the ninth century. At the end of century one band had established itself on the Mediterranean coast at Le Freinet (Fraxinetum) in Provence. From this highly fortified position they went about preying on pilgrims and merchants who traveled across the Alps to and from Italy (3B, 5M, 11E, 15E, 21G, 22H, 33I). In addition, they conducted plundering raids into neighboring territories (18D). Flodoard revels in the successful Byzantine naval assault on the Saracens at Le Freinet in 933 (13B) and takes note that King Hugh of Italy attacked their base in 942 (24C). However, it was not until after Flodoard's account ends that William of Arles destroyed this Muslim base (973).

The "Feudal Revolution"

The era in which Flodoard lived and wrote has been seen as very important in the institutional, social, and economic history of France in particular, but also of western Europe in general. The dominant historical view until about 1950 was that the invasions and disorders of the ninth century led to a breakdown of central institutions, with the years 860-90 being the most decisive ones in the transition from the effective and highly centralized Carolingian govern-ment to the fragmented and decentralized "feudal" world of the eleventh cen-tury in which the state as an entity collapsed. In this view, the tenth century represented the first full century of this disordered and chaotic period.

However, from the 1950s and continuing throughout the last half of the twentieth century, a number of scholars have argued that the last few decades of the tenth century and the first three decades of the eleventh century were marked by a significant change in society. This change could be seen in the devolution of power down to the level of holders of castles, who, backed by their own virtual private armies of mounted men (knights), were able to impose their own authority and financial exactions on the peasants of their locales while usurping the institutions of justice for their own benefit. To these scholars, the tenth century was seen as the last period of the "good old days" of order and public power before their collapse around the year 1000.

This transition, many have argued, is so significant that it can justly be termed a "feudal mutation" or "feudal revolution." A new twist was added in the 1990s when it was suggested that this "revolution" was also marked by the new lords' use of violence to impose their regimes on the surrounding popu-lace. Importantly, events recorded in Flodoard's *Annals* have been offered as evidence of this development.[21]

This putative "feudal revolution" has not gone unchallenged. A number of historians have responded forcefully that many of the observed changes pertain only to isolated and peripheral regions of France, or that they represent only semantic changes in the documentation or, indeed, that the observed new trends were not new at all but had been present all along.[22] The debate contin-ues and Flodoard's *Annals* represent an important body of source material for considering the state of royal power, the position of local authorities, and the nature of society in the middle half of the tenth century.

The Translation

This translation is based on the critical edition of Flodoard's Latin text estab-lished by Philippe Lauer in *Les Annales de Flodoard*.[23] While Flodoard began each annual entry with the year of the Incarnation with December 25 marking the beginning of the year, he also concluded each year with a Greek number, so that his first year, 919, carried the number KΣ (27), 920 was numbered KZ (28), all the way to 965, which was numbered OΓ (73). These are truncated forms of the Byzantine calendar, which numbered years from the year of creation, dated to 5509 BC in modern reckoning. Thus when the year 919 began for Flodoard (25 December 918), the Annus Mundi was 6426 (ΣYKZ, which began 1 September 918), shortened to KΣ (26) by Flodoard, and so on sequentially throughout the *Annals*.[24] We have omitted this numbering system and replaced the Greek numbers with Arabic numerals beginning with 1 for 919, the first year of the *Annals*, and progressing through to 48 for the year 966.

The division of Lauer's paragraphs has been retained when useful, but often they are extremely long and contain information on a variety of topics. Therefore we have subdivided most of Lauer's long paragraphs into smaller, more thematically unified paragraphs. The designation of these paragraphs by capital Roman letters (A, B, C, etc.) is thus our own.

For a great many technical and debatable Latin terms we have retained the Latin forms rather than translate them into English, which would often be confusing or require the use of different English terms for the same Latin word depending on circumstances. For example, Flodoard used a number of terms for fortifications, such as *castrum*, *castellum* and *munitio*, for which there are no single English equivalents. Rather than simply translating them all as "fortification," we have left them in Latin so that readers can note the variety of language employed by Flodoard. We have provided a glossary of these terms following the translation. At the same time, however, we have translated a number of Flodoard's technical terms and phrases into English (for example *miles* as soldier, *fidelis* as faithful follower), and we have provided Flodoard's Latin word in brackets so that the reader will not be in doubt concerning Flodoard's own terminology.

Notes to the Introduction

1 Jean Dunbabin, *France in the Making, 843-1180* (Oxford, New York, Toronto: Oxford University Press, 1985) 17.

2 Rosamond McKitterick, "The Carolingian Kings and the See of Rheims, 883-987," *Ideal and Reality in Frankish and Anglo-Saxon Society, Studies Presented to J.M. Wallace-Hadrill*, ed. Patrick Wormald, with Donald Bullough and Roger Collins (Oxford: Basil Blackwell, 1983) 228, and see 228-48 generally for Reims in the tenth century.

3 See below, ix, x, and xvi.

4 McKitterick, "Carolingian Kings," 229-31.

5 McKitterick, "Carolingian Kings," 234-35, 238.

6 McKitterick, "Carolingian Kings," 245.

7 McKitterick, "Carolingian Kings," 240; Franz Brunhölzl, *Histoire le la littérature latine du moyen âge*, trans. Henri Rochais, vol. 2 (Louvain: Brepols, 1996) 111-12.

8 *Carolingian Chronicles: Royal Frankish Annals and Nithard's Histories*, trans. Bernhard Walter Scholz, with Barbara Rogers (Ann Arbor: University of Michigan Press, 1972) 5, 20-21.

9 *The Annals of St-Bertin*, trans. Janet Nelson (Manchester and New York: Manchester University Press, 1991) 9-11. For a brief summary of Hincmar's importance, see Janet Nelson, *Charles the Bald* (London and New York: Longman, 1992) 145-46, and see Eleanor Shipley Duckett, *Carolingian Portraits, A Study in the Ninth Century* (Ann Arbor: University of Michigan, 1969) 202-64.

10 Here and throughout the Introduction, the number and letter refer to the entry subdivisions of the translated text of Flodoard.

11 Brunhölzl, *Histoire le la littérature latine*, 114-16.

12 Philippe Lauer, *Le règne de Louis IV d'Outre-Mer* (Paris: Émile Bouillon, 1900; repr. Geneva: Slatkine Reprints; Paris: Honoré Champion, 1977) 67; Flodoard, *Historia Remensis Ecclesiae* 4.28.

13 On Francia, see the Glossary.

14 The basic modern work on Flodoard as an historian is Michel Sot, *Un historien et son Église au Xe siècle* (Paris: Fayard, 1993). Also of great importance is the monographic work of Peter Christian Jacobsen, *Flodoard von Reims: sein Leben und seine Dichtung "De triumphis Christi"* (Leiden: Brill, 1978). Articles that should also be consulted include Harald von Zimmermann, "Zu Flodoards Historiographie und Regestentechnik," *Festschrift für Helmut Beumann zum 65 Geburtstag*, ed. Kurt-Ulrich Jäschke and R. Wenskus (Sigmaringen: Thorbecke, 1977); Martina Stratmann, "Die *Historia Remensis Ecclesiae*: Flodoards Umgang mit seinen Quellen," *Filologia Mediolatina: Rivista della Fondazione Franceschini* 1 (1994): 111-27; Françoise Châtillon, "La double sincérité de Flodoard," *Revue du Moyen Age Latin* 36 (1980): 89-94; Françoise Châtillon, "Pour relecture de Flodoard," *Revue du Moyen Age Latin* 37 (1981): v-xxxvii. Several of the articles published in *La Storiografia Altomedievale: Settimane di Studio de Centro Italiano sull'alto Medioevo* 17 (Spoleto, 1970) are of exceptional value. These include F.L. Ganshof, "L'Historiographie dans la monarchie franque sous les Mérovingiens et les Carolingiens," 631-85; Robert-Henri Bautier, "L'Historiographie en France aux Xe et XIe siècles (France du Nord et de l'Est)," 793-850; and Edmond-René Labande, "L'Historiographie en France de la ouest aux Xe et XIe siècles," 751-91.

15 A quasi-adoption, not a real one, for which there were no precedents.

16 Louis was the son of Eadgifu, sister of Hugh's wife Eadhild; on the marriages of the daughters of King Edward the Elder of England, see p. xxvi.

17 See the Glossary.

18 Brother of Louis IV (31A).

19 Liudprand of Cremona, *Antapodosis*, 4.13, *The Embassy to Constantinople and Other Writings*, trans. F.A. Wright, ed. John Julius Norwich (London: J.M. Dent; Rutland, VT: Charles E. Tuttle, 1993) 108.

20 Liudprand of Cremona, *Antapodosis*, 6.2, *The Embassy to Constantinople and Other Writings*, 151-52.

21 T.N. Bisson, "The 'Feudal Revolution,'" *Past and Present* 142 (February 1994): 6-42, and 10, 13, 25 for the references to Flodoard.

22 On this general debate, see especially the series of articles published in *Past and Present*: Bisson, "Feudal Revolution," 6-42; Dominique Barthélemy, "Debate: The 'Feudal Revolution,' Comment 1," 152 (August 1996): 196-205; Stephen D. White, "Debate: The 'Feudal Revolution,' Comment 2," 152 (August 1996): 205-23; Timothy Reuter, "Debate: The 'Feudal Revolution,' Comment 3," 155 (May 1997): 177-95; Chris Wickham, "Debate: The 'Feudal Revolution,' Comment 4," 155 (May 1997): 196-208; T.N. Bisson, "Debate: The 'Feudal Revolution,' Reply," 155 (May 1997): 208-25.

23 Paris: Alphonse Picard et Fils, 1905.

24 Lauer, *Annales de Flodoard*, lx-lxiv.

Bibliography

A. Texts and Translations of Flodoard

Annalium et historiae Francorum scriptores coaetanei XII. Ed. Pierre Pithou. Paris, 1588. 147-286; Frankfort, 1594. 109-213.

Historiae Francorum Scriptores. Ed. André Du Chesne. Vol. 2. Paris: S. Cramoisy, 1636. 590-623.

Recueil des Historiens des Gaules et de la France, vol. 8. Ed. Martin Bouquet. Paris: 1752. 176-215.

Patrologia Latina (Patrologiae cursus completus: seu bibliotheca universalis, integra, uniformis, commoda, oeconomica, omnium SS. Patrum, doctorum scriptorumque ecclesiasticorum sive latinorum sive graecorum qui ab aevo apostolico ad Innocentium III floruerunt: series Latina, in qua prodeunt Patres, doctores scriptoresque Ecclesiae Latinae, a Tertulliano ad Innocentium III. Ed. J.-P. Migne. Paris: Garnier Fratres, 1884-1905), vol. 135, cols. 423-89.

Monumenta Germaniae Historica: Scriptores, vol. 13. Ed. J. Heller and G. Waitz. Hannover, 1881. 368-408.

Chronique de Frodoard (sic). Trans. M. Guizot. In *Collection des Mémoires relatifs à l'Histoire de France*, vol. 6. Paris: J.-L.-J. Brière, 1824. 67-162.

Chronique de Flodoard. Trans. Clair Bandeville. Reims, 1855.

Les Annales de Flodoard. Ed. Philippe Lauer. Collection des textes pour servir à l'enseignement de l'histoire, vol. 39. Paris: Alphonse Picard et Fils, 1905.

B. Sources

The Annals of St-Bertin. Trans. Janet Nelson. Manchester and New York: Manchester University Press, 1991.

Carolingian Chronicles, Royal Frankish Annals and Nithard's Histories. Trans. Bernhard Walter Scholz with Barbara Rogers. Ann Arbor: University of Michigan Press, 1972.

Flodoard. *Historia Remensis Ecclesia.* Ed. I. Heller and G. Waitz. *Monumenta Germaniae Historica: Scriptores.* Vol. 13. Hannover: Hahn, 1881. 405-599.

_____. *Flodoard von Reims, Die Geschichte der Reimser Kirche.* Ed. Martina Stratmann. *Monumenta Germaniae Historica: Scriptores.* Vol. 36. Hannover: Hahnsche Buchhandlung, 1998.

Liudprand of Cremona. *The Embassy to Constantinople and Other Writings.* Ed. John Julius Norwich. Trans. F.A. Wright. London: J.M. Dent, and Rutland, VT: Charles E. Tuttle, 1993.

Recueil des Actes de Lothaire et de Louis V, rois de France (954-987). Ed. Louis Halphen and Ferdinand Lot. Chartes et diplômes de France publiés par les soins de l'Académie des inscriptions et belles-lettres. Paris: C. Klincksieck, 1908.

Recueil des Actes de Louis IV, roi de France (936-954). Ed. Maurice Prou and Philippe Lauer. Chartes et diplômes de France publiés par les soins de l'Académie des inscriptions et belles-lettres. Paris: C. Klincksieck, 1914.

Richer. *Histoire de France (888-995).* 2 vols. Ed. Robert Latouche. Paris: Société d'Édition "Les Belles Lettres," 1967.

Widukind of Corvey. *Widukindi Monachi Corbeinsis Rerum Gestarum Saxonicarum Libri Tres.* Ed. G. Waitz and K.A. Kehr. 5th ed. Hannover: Hahnsche Buchhandlung, 1935.

C. Scholarly Works

Barthélemy, Dominique. "Debate: The 'Feudal Revolution,' Comment 1." *Past and Present* 152 (August 1996): 196-205.

Bates, David. *Normandy Before 1066.* London and New York: Longman, 1982.

_____. "West Francia: the northern principalities." *The New Cambridge Medieval History.* Vol. 3. Ed. Timothy Reuter. Cambridge: Cambridge University Press, 1999. 398-419.

Bautier, Robert-Henri. "L'Historiographie en France aux Xe et XIe siècles (France du Nord et de l'Est)." In *La Storiografia Altomedievale: Settimane di Studio de Centro Italiano sull'alto Medioevo.* Vol. 17. Spoleto: Presso la Sede del Centro, 1970. 793-850.

Bisson, T.N. "The 'Feudal Revolution.'" *Past and Present* 142 (February 1994): 6-42.

_____. "Debate: The 'Feudal Revolution,' Reply." *Past and Present* 155 (May 1997): 208-25.

Bouchard, Constance Brittain. "Burgundy and Provence." *The New Cambridge Medieval History*. Vol. 3. Ed. Timothy Reuter. Cambridge: Cambridge University Press, 1999. 328-45.

Boussard, Jacques. "Les origines des comtés de Tours, Blois et Chartres." *Actes du 103e Congrès national de Sociétés savantes*. Paris: Bibliothèque Nationale, 1979. 85-112.

Brunhölzl, Franz. *Histoire le la littérature latine du moyen âge*. Vol. 2. Trans. Henri Rochais. Brepols: Louvain, 1996.

Bur, Michel. *La formation du comté de Champagne, v. 950–v. 1150*. Nancy: Université de Nancy II, 1977.

Châtillon, Françoise. "La double sincérité de Flodoard." *Revue du Moyen Age Latin*. Vol. 36 (1980): 89-94.

Christophersen, Paul. "The Spoken Word in International Contacts in Carolingian Europe." *NOWELE [North-western European Language Evolution]* 20 (1992): 53-64.

_____. "Pour relecture de Flodoard." *Revue du Moyen Age Latin* 37 (1981): v-xxxvii.

Dhondt, Jan. *Études sur la naissance des principautés territoriales en France (IXe-Xe siècle)*. Bruges: De Tempel, 1948.

Duckett, Eleanor Shipley. *Carolingian Portraits, A Study in the Ninth Century*. Ann Arbor: University of Michigan Press, 1969.

_____. *Death and Life in the Tenth Century*. Ann Arbor: University of Michigan Press, 1971.

Dunbabin, Jean. "West Francia: the kingdom." *The New Cambridge Medieval History*. Vol. 3. Ed. Timothy Reuter. Cambridge: Cambridge University Press, 1999. 372-97.

Ganshof, F. L. "À propos de ducs et de duchés au haut moyen âge." *Journal des savants* (Jan-Mar 1972): 13-24.

_____. "L'Historiographie dans la monarchie franque sous les Mérovingiens et les Carolingiens." *La Storiografia Altomedievale: Settimane di Studio de Centro Italiano sull'alto Medioevo*. Vol. 17. Spoleto: Presso la Sede del Centro, 1970. 631-85.

Jacobsen, Peter Christian. *Flodoard von Reims: sein Leben und seine Dichtung "De triumphis Christi."* Leiden: Brill, 1978.

Kurth, Godofroid. *Notger de Liège et la civilisation au Xe siècle*. Vol. 1. Brussels: Oscar Schepens, Liège: Louis Demarteau, 1905.

Labande, Edmond-René. "L'Historiographie en France de la ouest aux Xe et XIe siècles." In *La Storiografia Altomedievale: Settimane di Studio de Centro Italiano sull'alto Medioevo*. Vol. 17. Spoleto: Presso la Sede del Centro, 1970. 751-91.

Lauer, Philippe. *Le règne de Louis IV d'Outre-Mer*. Paris: Émile Bouillon, 1900; repr. Geneva: Slatkine Reprints; Paris: Honoré Champion, 1977.

Lewis, Andrew W. *Royal Succession in Capetian France: Studies on Familial Order and the State*. Cambridge, MA, and London: Harvard University Press, 1981.

Lot, Ferdinand. *Les derniers Carolingiens, Lothaire, Louis V, Charles de Lorraine, 954-991*. Paris: Émile Bouillon, 1891; repr. Geneva: Slatkine Reprints; Paris: Honoré Champion, 1975.

Lusse, Jackie. *Naissance d'une cité Laon et le Laonnois du Ve au Xe siècle*. Nancy: Presses Universitaires de Nancy, 1992.

Matossian, Mary Kilbourne. "Mold Poisoning and Population Growth in England and France, 1750-1850." *Journal of Economic History* 44 (1984): 669-86.

_____. *Poisons of the Past*. New Haven and London: Yale University Press, 1989.

McKitterick, Rosamond. "The Carolingian Kings and the See of Rheims, 883-987." *Ideal and Reality in Frankish and Anglo-Saxon Society, Studies Presented to J. M. Wallace-Hadrill*. Ed. Patrick Wormald, with Donald Bullough and Roger Collins. Oxford: Basil Blackwell, 1983. 228-48.

_____. *The Frankish Kingdoms Under the Carolingians, 751-987*. London and New York: Longman, 1983.

Müller-Mertens, Eckhard. "The Ottonians as kings and emperors." *The New Cambridge Medieval History*. Vol. 3. Ed. Timothy Reuter. Cambridge: Cambridge University Press, 1999. 233-66.

Nelson, Janet. *Charles the Bald*. London and New York: Longman, 1992.

Nicholas, David. *Medieval Flanders*. London and New York: Longman, 1992.

Parisse, Michel. "Lotharingia." *The New Cambridge Medieval History*. Vol. 3. Ed. Timothy Reuter. Cambridge: Cambridge University Press, 1999. 310-27.

Reuter, Timothy. "Debate: The 'Feudal Revolution,' Comment 3." *Past and Present* 155 (May 1997): 177-95.

Sassier, Yves. "Thibaud le Tricheur et Hugues le Grand." *Pays de Loire et Aquitaine de Robert le Fort aux premiers Capétiens*. Ed Olivier Guillot and Robert Favreau. *Mémoires de la Société des Antiquaires de l'Ouest*. 5th ser. Vol. 4 (1996): 145-57.

Schwager, Helmut. *Graf Heribert II. von Soissons, Omois, Meaux, Madrie sowie Vermandois (900/06-943) und die Francia (Nord-Frankreich) in der 1. Hälfte des 10. Jahrhunderts*. Münchener Historische Studien, Abteilung Mittlalterliche Geschichte. Ed. Eduard Hlawitschka. Vol. 6. Munich: Verlag Michael Lassleben Kallmünz, 1994.

Sot, Michel. *Un historien et son Église au Xe siècle*. Paris: Fayard, 1993.

Stratmann, Martina. "Die *Historia Remensis Ecclesiae*: Flodoards Umgang mit seinen Quellen." *Filologia Mediolatina: Rivista della Fondazione Franceschini* 1 (1994): 111-27.

Werner, Karl Ferdinand. "Königtum und Fürstentum des französischen 12. Jahrhunderts." In *Probleme des 12. Jahrhunderts*. Sigmaringen: Jan Thorbecke Verlag, 1968. 177-225. Repr. as "Kingdom and principality in twelfth-century France." *The Medieval Nobility. Studies on the ruling classes of France and Germany from the sixth to the twelfth century*. Ed. and trans. Timothy Reuter. Amsterdam, New York and Oxford: North Holland Publishing, 1978.

_____. "La genèse des duchés en France et en Allemagne." In *Nascita dell'Europa ed Europa carolingia: un'equazione da verificare*. Settimane di Studio del Centro Italiano di Studi sull'Alto Medioevo. Vol. 27. Spoleto: Presso la Sede del Centro, 1981.

175-207.

White, Stephen D. "Debate: The 'Feudal Revolution,' Comment 2." *Past and Present* 152 (August 1996): 205-23.

Wickham, Chris, "Debate: The 'Feudal Revolution,' Comment 4." *Past and Present* 155 (May 1997): 196-208.

Zimmermann, Harald von. "Zu Flodoards Historiographie und Regestentechnik." In *Festschrift für Helmut Beumann zum 65. Geburtstag.* Ed. Kurt-Ulrich Jäschke and R. Wenskus. Sigmaringen: Thorbecke, 1977. 81-95.

Zimmermann, Michael. "Western Francia: the southern principalities." *The New Cambridge Medieval History.* Vol. 3. Ed. Timothy Reuter. Cambridge: Cambridge University Press, 1999. 420-55.

THE ANNALS OF FLODOARD

I.

In the year 919 from the incarnation of our Lord Jesus Christ, a marvelous hailstone fell at Reims. It was larger than a hen's egg and was wider than half a person's palm. However, even larger hail was seen to have fallen in certain other places. This year there was no wine in the *pagus* of Reims, or much too little. The Northmen ravaged, destroyed and annihilated all of Brittany in Cournouaille,[1] which is located on the seashore. The Bretons were abducted and sold, while those who escaped were driven out. The Magyars raided Italy and part of Francia, that is, Lothair's Kingdom.[2]

2.

[2A] In the year 920 from the Lord's incarnation, almost all the counts of Francia gathered at the *urbs* of Soissons and abandoned their king Charles. This was done because Charles was unwilling to dismiss his counselor Hagano, a man of middling origins whom Charles had raised to power. However, Heriveus, the archbishop of Reims, received the king after they all had deserted him and led the king to his house in the *villa* of Chacrise. Indeed, on the next day they came to Crugny, a *villa* belonging to the diocese of Reims, where they stayed until they moved on to Reims. Thus Heriveus settled Charles for almost seven

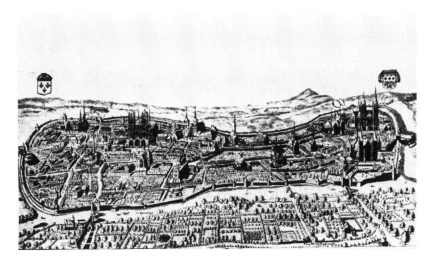

Fig. I. Reims in the Seventeenth Century (an engraving of 1622)
The cathedral (constructed in the thirteenth century) is on the left; on the right front is the church of the abbey of St-Rémi (constructed in the eleventh century). In the tenth century, the quarter of St-Rémi was enclosed by its own walls.
From *Reims and the Battles for its Possession* (Clermont-Ferrand: Michelin & Cie, 1919) 7.

months until he might be able to restore the king's *principes* and his kingdom to him.

[2B] Afterwards, Archbishop Heriveus set out on the Meuse to regain a certain *castellum*, called Mézières, located in the territory of his own diocese, which Count Erlebaldus of the *pagus* of Châtresais was holding against Heriveus. Erlebaldus had been excommunicated by the archbishop because of the evils that he had frequently inflicted on the dependents (*familia*) of that diocese. Moreover, he had violently seized the *castrum* of Omont, which belonged to the church of Reims. However, after the archbishop and his *fideles* had besieged Mézières for nearly four weeks, they took it after Erlebaldus abandoned it. Heriveus stationed a garrison (*custodii*) there and then returned to Reims. Erlebaldus proceeded to the king, who was then delaying in the *pagus* of Worms, encamped against Henry, the Transrhenish *princeps*.[3] There Erlebaldus was surprised and killed by enemies of the king.

[2C] This year and also in the next year [921], a quarrel over the diocese of Tongres arose between Bishop Hilduinus and Abbot Richarius [of Prüm]. Earlier, the king [Charles] had given that diocese to Richarius because Hilduinus, to whom he had previously conceded the bishopric, had been unfaithful to him. Both the clergy and people had elected Hilduinus bishop and Archbishop Herimannus [of Cologne] had ordained him bishop there, and Gislebert,[4] whom most of the Lotharingians had chosen as their *princeps* when King Charles had been abandoned [by his magnates], also had given his agreement. In fact, when the Lotharingians and this Gislebert had brought themselves back to him, King Charles agreed that the diocese of Tongres should go to Abbot Richarius and not to Bishop Hilduinus.

[2D] At Reims, at the door of the basilica of the monastery of Saint Peter, a wax taper that had been placed there by the townsmen (*cives*) who had set out for Rome to visit the tombs of the apostles, was ignited miraculously three times by heavenly fire. Also a certain girl, named Osanna, from the *pagus* of Voncq, came to the monastery. She had not consumed meat nor had she been able to eat bread for two years. Many visions were shown to her. At this time she lay unmoving for a full week and, to the amazement of all, she sweated blood. Her entire forehead and her face down to her neck were covered in blood, yet some life and warmth remained in her as she breathed shallow breaths. When she was roused she maintained that she had seen many things, some of which she revealed but most she said that she dare not say. Then, around the *urbs* of Reims, honey was found in spikes of grain and flowers were found in certain mature trees and in fruit already collected.

3.

[3A] In the year 921 of the Incarnate Word, Bishop Raoul [I] of the Mount of Laon[5] died. He was succeeded by Adelelmus, the treasurer of the same place, who was ordained at Reims by Lord Bishop Heriveus.

[3B] Many of the English set out for Rome and were killed by stones in the defiles of the Alps by the Saracens.

[3C] A synod was held at Trosly-Loire, presided over by Archbishop Heriveus and attended by King Charles. The king interceded on behalf of Erlebaldus, who was then absolved of his excommunication at Châtresais.

[3D] Richard [the Justiciar], *marchio* of Burgundy, died.

[3E] King Charles went into Lothair's Kingdom and retook by force certain fortifications (*praesidia*) of Ricuinus, who was unfaithful to Charles. After a pact was made with Henry, the Transrhenish *princeps*, which was to last until the feast of Saint Martin [11 November], he returned to the Mount of Laon.

[3F] In this year there were many storms in different places. Men were killed by lightning and homes were burned. There was great heat during the summer and much hay was produced. There was a great drought for almost three straight months, in July, August and September.

[3G] For five months Count Robert [of Paris][6] besieged the Northmen who were operating on the river Loire. After he received hostages from them, he conceded Brittany to the Northmen, which they had devastated, along with the *pagus* of Nantes. The Northmen began to take up the faith of Christ.

[3H] Erluinus, bishop of Beauvais, died.

[3I] Again King Charles confirmed the peace with Henry [king of Germany].[7]

4.

[4A] In the year 922, in the prosecution of Gislebert and Otho,[8] Charles laid waste to Lothair's Kingdom with rapine, sacrileges and fires, even campaigning in the season of Lent[9] and for the entire winter. Richarius, who had set out for Rome on the matter of the bishopric of Tongres,[10] returned after having been ordained by Pope John [X], who had excommunicated Hilduinus and dismissed him as bishop. Drogo, bishop of Toul, died and Goslenus succeeded him.[11]

[4B] King Berengar of the Lombards was deprived of his power (*regnum*) by the magnates (*optimates*), because of his insolence, and they admitted Rudolf, the king of Cisalpine Gaul,[12] into power. As a result of the actions of the aforesaid Berengar,[13] the Magyars plundered Italy and captured many *oppida*.

[4C] Charles returned to Laon and, after Easter [21 April], Hugh [the Great], the son of [Count] Robert came across the Vesle to the *villa* of Fismes, where he met with *fideles* of Archbishop Heriveus [of Reims], along with certain of the counts of Francia. Hugh set out with these men on the river Aisne in the *pagus* of Laon on account of Hagano, to whom the king had given the abbey of Chelles, which had belonged to Rothildis, Charles's aunt and the mother-in-law of Hugh.[14] Charles secretly departed from Laon, along with Heribert [of Vermandois] and Hagano, because of his love for Hagano, and set out across the Meuse because of his fear. Hugh, with 2000 other fighting men (*pugnatores*), followed Charles across the Meuse and met there with Gislebert the Lotharingian. Hugh returned with Gislebert and was summoned to a meeting by his father [Robert], who had followed him and was encamped on the Aisne in the *pagus* of Laon. When Charles learned of this, he recrossed the Meuse with many Lotharingians who had joined him and he began to raid and burn *villae* of the church of Reims. By military action Charles took and made indefensible the *castrum* of Omont, but his own troops suffered considerable losses. Therefore, [Count] Robert proceeded to the Marne to meet Raoul, the son of Richard [the Justiciar] and his own son-in-law.[15] Charles followed him and crossed the Marne with the Lotharingians, while the confederates of Hagano captured the *castrum* of Épernay. When Raoul arrived with the Burgundians, [Count] Robert crossed the river [Marne] below Épernay and laid out his fortified camp (*castra*) not more than three leagues from the army of Charles. There both Robert and Raoul remained encamped for more than a week and met in a conference without Hagano and Charles.

[4D] Meanwhile, Hugh [the Black], the son of Richard [the Justiciar], came to [Count] Robert and attacked about 200 men who had been in alliance with Hagano [and] who were setting out to plunder *villae* of the diocese of Reims. Some of the men were captured and three were killed. He led off some horses and captured some weapons. He sent back the surviving prisoners to their own people, burdened with shame. After these events transpired, Robert and King Charles laid out their camps, the former at Chaumuzy and the latter in the vicinity of Reims, a league away from the *civitas*. There Charles's forces sat for three straight days, with many of their horses being captured by the townsmen (*cives*) of Reims. In response, Charles's forces attacked the *urbs* even though it was Pentecost Sunday [9 June]. As a result many of the Lotharingians were killed and many others were wounded before night ended the battle. Finally, it was heard that those who were with Robert had captured Laon and that Hagano's treasures that were in the city had been scattered and that Robert's men had seized one of Hagano's brothers. Charles and Hagano then advanced on Laon. Some of the Lotharingians returned home but others continued on with Charles. Robert had pitched his tents on the river Alette. Charles, denied an entry to Laon, settled on the river Serre. Each day Robert's forces increased while those of Charles diminished. Finally Charles secretly withdrew with Hagano and set out across the Meuse.

[4E] The Franks chose Robert as their lord (*senior*) and committed themselves to him. Thus Robert was established as king at Reims, at [the monastery of] St-Rémi, by the bishops and magnates (*primates*) of the kingdom. Heriveus, the [arch]bishop of Reims, died on the third day after the consecration of King Robert, that is, on 2 July, on the fourth day before he would have completed the twenty-second year of his episcopate. He was succeeded as archbishop of Reims by Seulfus, who was then holding the office of archdeacon in Reims.

[4F] At Cambrai it seemed that three suns appeared, or that the sun had three orbs equally distant from each other. Likewise two sun rays appeared on opposite sides of the sun but in close proximity to it until they were covered by a cloud. Likewise two beams of light were close together in the sky until they, too, were covered by a cloud.[16]

[4G] [King] Robert sent his son Hugh [the Great] into Lothair's Kingdom with a military force (*agmen*) of the Franks to free from investment Gislebert's *castrum* of Chièvremont, to which Charles was laying siege. When Charles learned of Hugh's approach, he raised the siege. Hugh received hostages from certain Lotharingians and returned to his father.

[4H] There was an earthquake in the *pagus* of Cambrésis, which threw down many houses there. In the *pagus* of Paris, in the *villa* of Juziers, it is remembered that many miracles were performed in the church of Saint Peter. These were due to the relics of the beard of Saint Peter that had been brought to the church four years earlier. Among the blind and lame and crippled, more than 170 returned home restored to health. Indeed, all those who had entered the church as demoniacs returned in good health with the demons having been defeated. Moreover, innumerable other things were done there.

5.

[5A] In the year 923 [King] Robert set out for Lothair's Kingdom to speak with King Henry [of Germany], who came to meet him in the *pagus* of the Ripuarians on the river Rur [Roer].[17] There they feared each other's power. After they had made a pact of friendship, they exchanged gifts and departed. At the same time, certain Lotharingians gave hostages and they received a truce from Robert that was to last until the first day of October.

[5B] The Northmen raided Aquitaine and the Auvergne. William, the duke of the Aquitanians, and Raymond [count of Toulouse] fought against them, and 12,000 of the Northmen were killed there.

[5C] [Count] Boso, the son of Richard [the Justiciar], killed Ricuinus [count of Verdun], who was confined to his bed.[18]

[5D] [King] Charles crossed the Meuse and came to Attigny, along with his

Lotharingians, who had broken the truce that they had recently received from [King] Robert. Before Robert was able to assemble his *fideles*, Charles and his forces suddenly arrived on the Aisne, where he learned that Robert was encamped beneath the *urbs* of Soissons. On the next day, a Sunday [15 June], after the sixth hour [noon] had passed, when the Franks were not expecting a battle that day and many of them were eating their meals, Charles crossed the Aisne and attacked Robert with the well armed Lotharingians who were with him. Robert, however, counterattacked Charles with his own well armed men. The battle began and many fell on each side. King Robert also died, pierced through by lances.

[5E] However, those who were on Robert's side, that is, his son Hugh [the Great] and Heribert [count of Vermandois] and others, were able to gain the victory. They forced Charles and his Lotharingians to retreat in flight. But because of the death of their king Robert they did not pursue the defeated, but rather they took control of their camp and seized spoils, especially from the country folk (*rusticani*) and from those who streamed out from the suburb of the *urbs* of Soissons. Finally, the Lotharingians lost many wagons to Count Roger [of Laon], who brought them into the *castrum* of Laon. The Lotharingians left Charles behind in the kingdom of Francia and they returned home.

[5F] Charles sent out many delegations to prevail upon Count Heribert [of Vermandois] and Archbishop Seulfus and the rest of the magnates (*primates*) of the kingdom to support him once again. They rejected his request and sent to Burgundy for Raoul,[19] who swiftly hurried to them with a large force of his own men. When the Franks heard that Charles had summoned the Northmen to come to him, they took up a position with Raoul between Charles and the Northmen on the river Oise, preventing them from joining forces. Then Charles fled back across the Meuse and all of them [the Franks] chose Raoul as king.

[5G] Raoul, the son of Richard [the Justiciar], was established as king at the *urbs* of Soissons.[20] Count Heribert [of Vermandois] directed his cousin Bernard,[21] along with other legates who were unaware of their plan, to go to Charles. Charles was persuaded by their oaths and set out to Heribert with a few of his men. Heribert received Charles in his own *castellum* of St-Quentin, on the Somme. Heribert sent away those who had come with Charles and had Charles taken to Château-Thierry, a *munitio* of his on the river Marne. There Heribert placed Charles in custody with the necessary provisions and then followed King Raoul into Burgundy.

[5H] Meanwhile, Ragenold, the *princeps* of the Northmen who were engaged on the river Loire, had for a long time been stirred up by Charles's frequent messages and now crossed the Oise and raided Francia, joined by many from Rouen. Heribert's *fideles* unexpectedly overcame the camp of the forces from Rouen, who had remained in their *castella*. Count Raoul [of Goucy], stepson of Roger [count of Laon], and Count Ingobrannus joined Heribert and they took great spoils and liberated from captivity 1000 prisoners there. When Ragenold learned this he was enraged and ravaged the *pagus* of Arras. Count Adelelmus [of Arras] came out to meet him and killed 600 of the invaders while the others slipped away in flight. Ragenold hurried with his men to take refuge in his *munitiones*, from where he continued carrying out plunderings and brigandage as he could.

[5I] Because of all of these actions, King Raoul was summoned from Burgundy to Compiègne, on the Oise, by Hugh [the Great], the son of [King] Robert. Upon hearing that the Northmen had plundered the *pagus* of Beauvais, Raoul crossed [the Oise to Beauvais], along with Archbishop Seulfus, Count Heribert [of Vermandois] and certain other select brave men. They crossed the Epte and entered the land that had been given to the Northmen when they had come to the faith of Christ shortly before, so that they might cultivate the faith and have peace. King Raoul and the Franks devastated part of this land with fire and sword because those Northmen had broken the peace which they had earlier agreed to with King Charles, who [now] promised them a vast expanse of land. Envoys from the Lotharingians went to Raoul, who was engaged in these operations, promising that they would place themselves and their possessions under him. Raoul was diverted from his campaign of devastation by this delegation and he went out to meet the Lotharingians on the advice of the magnates (*primates*) who were with him. He left Count Hugh [the Great] and Count Heribert [of Vermandois] behind across [the east bank of] the Oise to protect the fatherland. Those Lotharingians came to meet Raoul at Mouzon.

[5J] Meanwhile, Raoul's wife Emma[22] was consecrated queen at Reims by Archbishop Seulfus. Raoul was elevated to power (*regnum*) by many Lotharingians and was asked by Bishop Wigeric of Metz to go to recapture the *castrum* of Saverne in the *pagus* of Alsace. He remained there for almost the entire autumn because the garrison (*castellani*), which was from across the Rhine, held out, vainly awaiting aid from [King] Henry. At last Raoul received hostages from them and returned to Laon to his wife.

[5K] Meanwhile, the Northmen raided certain of our *pagi* across the Oise, and our people raided their land. After numerous embassies passed back and forth, the Northmen promised to make peace with Count Heribert [of Vermandois], Archbishop Seulfus and the other Franks who were were encamped with them against the Northmen. This was on the condition that the more spacious land beyond the Seine, which they had requested, would be given to them. In the meantime, as was said, King Raoul returned to Laon, and the

Northmen sent hostages and accepted a truce from the king to last until the middle of May.

[5L] As these things were happening, it became known that Henry [king of Germany], at the invitation of Count Gislebert [of Lotharingia] and [Arch]bishop Roger of Trier, who had not yet submitted themselves to [King] Raoul, crossed the Rhine and raided Lothair's Kingdom. He laid waste the area between the Rhine and the Moselle, carried off herds and plow animals, drained away other resources and captured many people, including youths. When Henry heard that Raoul was gathering an army not only from Francia but also from all Burgundy, he retired into his own kingdom after agreeing to a truce with the Lotharingians to last until the first day of October of the following year. However, Otho [count of Verdun][23] deserted to Henry, along with those who had committed themselves to Raoul. Bishop Wigeric [of Metz] destroyed Saverne after recapturing it. Cambrai was set ablaze as a result of a fire that was not watched carefully. Rodulf, the king of Cisalpine Gaul,[24] whom the Italians had received into royal power (*regnum*) after their king Berengar had been deposed, fought against Berengar and defeated him. It is said that 1,500 men fell in that battle.

[5M] The archiepiscopal woolen band, which is called the *pallium*, was sent to Archbishop Seulfus by Pope John [X]. A large number of English, who were seeking the tomb of Saint Peter for the sake of prayer, were slaughtered in the Alps by the Saracens. Bishop Dado of Verdun died, and his bishopric was ceded to Hugh by King Raoul; this priest was consecrated bishop at Reims by [Arch]bishop Seulfus.

6.

[6A] Early in the year 924, a tax in money was collected throughout Francia, which was handed over to the Northmen for a pact of peace.[25] King Raoul prepared a journey into Aquitaine because William [II], the *princeps* of that region, had delayed making his personal submission. When William learned that Raoul was hurrying into Aquitaine with a hostile force, he came to meet him on the Loire. With representatives from each side going back and forth, at last William and Raoul met on the Loire, in the *pagus* of Autun. There they remained the whole day, with Raoul on this bank of the river and William on that bank as messengers traveled back and forth. Thus as the entire day passed, William finally crossed the river and came to Raoul at night. William vaulted from his horse and, on foot, approached the king, who was mounted on his horse. The king kissed him on both cheeks and he departed. On the next day, William returned to the king and they both agreed to a truce of eight days. After a week had passed, William committed himself to the king and the king restored to William the *pagus* of Berry. Earlier Raoul, assisted by Robert [count of Paris], who had not yet been made king, had taken it and the *civitas* of Bourges away from William by force. Raoul gave Péronne to Heribert [of Vermandois] and Le Mans to Hugh [the Great], [King] Robert's son. Archbishop Seulfus regained the adjacent land of St-Rémi in the province of Lyon from Hugh of Vienne,[26] who had been present at the same meeting. [Arch]bishop Heriveus [of Reims] had held nothing of this land.

[6B] Having returned from there, we[27] came to the *castellum* of Mont-St-Jean, which Ragenardus[28] had invaded and held. However, at the urging of his nephews Walo and Gislebert[29] and others whom the king had sent to retake the stronghold, Ragenardus sent his son to the king as a hostage. The king, at the urging of Ragenardus's kinsmen and of his own brother Hugh [the Black], ordered that the hostage be received and granted a truce to Ragenardus. All the others who were with Ragenardus he left bound to him by an oath.

[6C] Meanwhile, Berengar,[30] who was married to the sister of Gislebert [of Lotharingia], captured his brother-in-law. When the sons of Ragenarius, who was Gislebert's brother, were given to Berengar as hostages, he released Gislebert. Upon his freedom, Gislebert repeatedly devastated the lands of Berengar and of his own brother Ragenarius and of Count Isaac [of Cambrai]. Afterwards, Gislebert sent envoys to King Raoul so that he might be received by the king. The king detested the perjuries and inconstancy of Gislebert and, with the counsel of his *fideles*, refused to receive him.

[6D] King Berengar [of Italy], rejected by the Lombards, led the Magyars as they devastated Italy.[31] They set fire to the rich and populous *urbs* of Pavia, destroying vast resources there. Forty-four churches were set afire and the bishop of that city [John], along with the bishop of Vercelli [Ragamfridus], who had been with him, was killed by the fire and the smoke. From the almost innumerable multitude of inhabitants of Pavia, only 200 are said to have survived. They gave the Magyars eight measures of silver gathered from the ashes in the remains of the city, thus ransoming the life and walls of the empty *civitas*. When this was completed, the Magyars crossed the steep ridges of the Alps and came into Gaul. Rudolf [II], the king of Cisalpine Gaul [Transjurane (Upper) Burgundy] and Hugh of Vienne,[32] closed them up in the passes of the Alps but the Magyars escaped from this inhospitable place through narrow mountain passes and entered Gothia. The two military commanders (*duces*) Raoul and Hugh, pursued the Magyars and struck down those whom they were able to find. Meanwhile, Berengar, the king of Italy, was killed by his own people.

[6E] Raoul, the king of Francia, held a *placitum* at Attigny, where he prepared an expedition into Lothair's Kingdom. However, he was struck down by a serious illness. As his strength returned, just as it seemed that he was recovering, he suffered a severe relapse. Many despaired for him and he asked to be taken to [the monastery of] St-Rémi at Reims. Raoul was generous and gave many gifts to monasteries of Francia and Burgundy, excluding his wife's share of their goods. He remained at St-Rémi for four weeks until his health returned, and finally he went to the *urbs* of Soissons before returning to Burgundy.

[6F] Henry [king of Germany] was in the lands bordering on the Sarmatians[33] when he, like Raoul, fell ill and was delayed for the entire summer. Meanwhile, a dispute arose between Gislebert [of Lotharingia] and his brother Ragenarius, as well as conflict between Otho and Boso.[34] The result was killings, fires and raids by both sides. The Northmen made a peace with the Franks by oaths, due to the efforts of Count Hugh [the Great],[35] Count Heribert [of Vermandois], and Archbishop Seulfus because King Raoul was absent. However, with the king's consent, more lands were conceded to the Northmen in a pact of peace, that is, Maine and the Bessin.[36]

[6G] In a surprise attack Count Isaac [of Cambrai] captured and burned a *castellum* of Bishop Stephen of Cambrai. In a sudden fire he also burned the tower of the citadel (*praesidium*) of Heribert, which was on the river Marne, where [King] Charles was being held [Château-Thierry]. Ragenoldus[37] with his Northmen laid waste the lands of Hugh [the Great], between the Loire and the Seine, because they had not yet been given possessions inside the Gauls.

[6H] In October a synod of the bishops of the province of Reims was held at Trosly-Loire, with Archbishop Seulfus [of Reims] presiding. Count Isaac [of Cambrai] came to the synod to make amends and to give satisfaction for the things that he had perpetrated against the church of Cambrai.[38] Isaac bound over a hundred pounds of silver and made peace with Bishop Stephen [of Cambrai] in the presence of [Count] Heribert [of Vermandois] and many other counts of Francia. King Raoul received the *castellum* of Mont-St-Jean, which Ragenardus [viscount of Auxerre] had reluctantly abandoned, and he again sought out Francia. William [II of Aquitaine] and Hugh [the Great], son of Robert, made a security pact for their lands with Ragenoldus, and Ragenoldus and his Northmen set out into Burgundy.

[6I] In this year there were many lightings of candles in different parts of Francia, with the light arising suddenly. Moreover, visions of the saints were shown to Ebrulfus, a certain priest living in the nearby small village of Mouzon. At Reims, in the church of Saint Mary,[39] on the feast of All Saints [1 November], a man who had been crippled for a long time with his calves drawn back to the hamstrings was healed by divine power and he stood up.

[6J] It was reported that the Magyars who were ravaging Gothia suffered a plague, which caused dysentery and swelling of their heads, and very few survived.

7.

[7A] When the year 925 began, Ragenoldus with his Northmen devastated Burgundy. Count Warnerius [of Troyes], Manasses,[40] Bishop Ansegisus [of Troyes], and Bishop Gozcelinus [of Langres] joined forces to opposed them at Mons Calaus[41] and killed more than 800 of the Northmen. However, Count Warnerius was captured and killed when the horse on which he was mounted was killed, and Bishop Ansegisus of Troyes was wounded. When King Raoul learned of this, he set out to Burgundy with certain soldiers from Francia, that is, those from the church of Reims, along with Bishop Abbo of Soissons and a few others who escorted him, including Count Heribert [of Vermandois]. When he collected a substantial number of soldiers from Burgundy, he advanced to the fortified camp of the Northmen on the river Seine, where there was a struggle fought on foot. When the Northmen saw that those who were with the king, that is, the greatest part of the army, made no effort either to capture their camp or even to dismount, they came out of their camp to fight. After suffering losses the Franks broke off the engagement and laid out their camp in a circular pattern two or three miles away from the camp of the Northmen. Hugh [the Great], the son of Robert, laid out his own camp on the opposite bank of the Seine. Thus from day to day the Franks were delaying establishing a close siege of the Northmen's encampment as they awaited ships to come from Paris. However, with the complicity of some of our men, as it is said, the Northmen broke out of their camp and sought the cover of a certain forest to shield their movement and some of our own men returned home.

[7B] When the Lenten fasts[42] were begun, Heribert [count of Vermandois] spoke with Gislebert [of Lotharingia] and then with Hugh [the Great], and then he summoned King Raoul from Burgundy. Raoul hurried to meet him and set out for Cambrai in order to meet the Lotharingians and Gislebert. However, these latter ones did not attend the *placitum* and came to Raoul on the Meuse. Gislebert and Otho[43] were made Raoul's supporters.

[7C] The Northmen from Rouen broke the treaty to which they had formerly agreed and laid waste the *pagus* of Beauvais and Amiens. The *civitas* of Amiens was burned because a fire had been poorly tended by the refugees, and Arras was burned in a fire that suddenly arose. The Northmen came to plunder Noyon and they set fire to its suburbs. The garrison troops (*castellani*) of Noyon came out with the inhabitants of the suburbs and drove off the Northmen, killing those whom they were able and freeing part of the suburb from the enemy. Meanwhile, the men of the Bessin raided the land of the Northmen on the other side of the Seine. When news of this came, the men of Paris, along with some the *fideles* of Hugh [the Great], son of Robert, and with the garrison troops (*oppidani*) of some of his *castella*, laid waste a part of the *pagus* of Rouen that was possessed by the Northmen on this side of the Seine. *Villae* were burned, animals were carried away and some of the Northmen were killed. Meanwhile, because little fodder was available for their horses, Count Heribert [of Vermandois] and a few of the Franks remained on the Oise in order to deny a crossing to the Northmen. When the Northmen learned of the devastation of their land, they rushed back home.

[7D] Finally Henry [king of Germany] crossed the Rhine and took by storm the *oppidum* of Zülpich, which was defended by Gislebert's *fideles*. Henry did not remain long in Lothair's Kingdom, but after taking hostages from Gislebert he returned home across the Rhine. Count Hilgaudus [II of Pontheiu] and other Franks who lived along the sea coast invaded and devastated areas bordering on their own lands that the Northmen had recently come to possess.

[7E] Meanwhile, [King] Raoul left Burgundy and came to Francia in order to prepare for war against the Northmen, and he issued a call to arms to the Franks. Therefore, when the expedition against the Northmen had begun, Heribert [of Vermandois], with the soldiers of the church of Reims, Count Arnulf[44] and other Franks from along the sea coast attacked a *praesidium* of the Northmen. In response, their *princeps* Rollo sent 1,000 Northmen from Rouen, in addition to the men of that *oppidum*. This *castrum*, which is located near the sea, is called Eu. The Franks surrounded it, breached the encircling outer wall, and broke down and climbed the inner wall. They took possession of the *oppidum*, killed all the horses and burned the *munitio*. A few of the defenders escaped and took up a position on an island nearby Eu. The Franks attacked and seized the island, which took longer than their capture of the *oppidum* [of Eu]. Some of the Northmen who had been fighting for their lives finally gave up and jumped into the water in order to swim to safety but were drowned. Others died by the swords of the Franks while still others killed themselves with their own spears. When all the Northmen were thus dead and much booty had been captured, the Franks returned home.

[7F] However King Raoul, along with Hugh [the Great] and the Burgundians, established his court in the *pagus* of Beauvais. At this same time, Archbishop Seulfus of Reims died, having completed three years and five days of his episcopal office. Count Heribert [of Vermandois] came to Reims and saw to it that both the vassals (*vassali*) and the clergy of this church respected his advice concerning the election of an archbishop.[45] Hugh [the Great], son of Robert, made a pact of security with the Northmen, but the lands of the sons Baldwin,[46] and those of Raoul de Gouy and Hilgaudus [count of Ponthieu] were excluded from the agreement.

[7G] The diocese of Reims was committed to Count Heribert [of Vermandois],[47] who managed it for his son Hugh, a small boy, it was said, not yet five years of age.[48] Bishop Abbo [of Soissons] went to Rome with envoys from Count Heribert.[49] All the Lotharingians committed themselves to Henry [king of Germany], who then conceded the diocese of Verdun to Bernuinus, the nephew of Bishop Dado [of Verdun]. Bernuinus was ordained bishop there after the priest Hugh, to whom [King] Raoul had given the diocese, was expelled.

8.

[8A] When the year 926 began, King Raoul, Count Heribert [of Vermandois] and some of the Franks who lived along the sea coast besieged the Northmen in the *pagus* of Arras, who were crowded together in a forest. After several days, the Northmen suddenly attacked the king's camp at night. Count Heribert came to the assistance of the king lest Raoul should be captured by the Northmen and there was fighting at the encampment, with some huts there being burned. The Northmen were repulsed by an attack from the [king's] camp and they retreated, although the king was wounded and Count Hilgaudus [of Ponthieu] was killed. It is said that 1,100 Northmen died in that battle. Raoul then returned to Laon, and the Northmen plundered the forest region as far as the *pagus* of Porcien.

[8B] Moreover, the Magyars crossed the Rhine and raged as far as the *pagus* of Voncq, taking booty and setting fires. There was an eclipse of the moon, in its fourteenth day, on 1 April, the Saturday of Easter,[50] and it became pale, with just a little light remaining, just like a two-day old moon. As dawn broke, the entire moon became the color of blood. For fear of the Magyars the body of St-Rémi and the relics of other saints were taken from their monasteries and brought to Reims, to be placed among the relics of Saint Walburgis, and many miracles were performed there.

[8C] A tax of money was collected publicly through Francia and Burgundy and was given to the Northmen, in accordance with a [new] peace treaty. Thus, after the money had been handed over, the peace was confirmed by a [mutual] oath. Thereupon the army of King Raoul and Count Heribert [of Vermandois] marched out from Francia and Burgundy across the Loire and received hostages from the *urbs* of Nevers, which was being defended against the king by the brother of [Duke] William [of Aquitaine].[51] The army then crossed into Aquitaine in pursuit of William, who had deserted from the king, and it pursued him until there was news that the Magyars had crossed the Rhine, which forced the army back to Francia.

[8D] In Rome, Hugh, son of Bertha,[52] was constituted king over Italy after King Rudolf [II] of Cisalpine Gaul [Upper Burgundy] had been expelled. Hugh traveled to that kingdom and married a woman even though his wife was still alive. This was after Burchard, the *princeps* of the Alamanni and father-in-law of this Rudolf, was killed by Bertha's sons.[53] Burchard had crossed the Alps with Rudolf in order to regain the kingdom of Italy for his son-in-law.

[8E] The priest Hugh[54] was expelled from Verdun and died. Ebrardus,[55] who came from across the Rhine, was sent into Lothair's Kingdom by Henry [king of Germany] in order to do justice, and he was able to unite in peace the Lotharingians [who were fighting among themselves]. Count Raoul [de Gouy], the son of Heiluidis, died. Not long afterwards his step-father Roger,[56] the count of the *pagus* of Laon, also died. Hugh [the Great], the son of Robert, married [Eadhild] a daughter of Edward [the Elder], the king of the English, and the sister of [Eadgyfu] the wife of [King] Charles [the Simple].

9.

[9A] In 927, a conflict arose between King Raoul and Count Heribert [of Vermandois]. Heribert had asked that his son Odo be given the county of Laon but the king conceded it to Roger, one of the sons of Roger.[57] At Reims in the month of March on a Sunday morning, a line of fire was seen in the sky. Following that sign a plague came, with fever and a cough in a mixed pestilence, which stole into all of the peoples of Germany and Gaul. Bishop Widricus of Metz died. Count Heribert sent his legates across the Rhine to Henry [king of Germany]. When they returned, they summoned Heribert to a meeting with [King] Henry. Heribert, along with Hugh [the Great], the son of Robert, hurried to the meeting and peace was made. Heribert and [King] Henry honored each other with gifts. At that time [King] Henry gave the diocese of Metz to Benno, God's servant, despite an election [of another] by the people of Metz.

[9B] Hugh [the Great], the son of Robert, and Count Heribert [of Vermandois] proceeded against the Northmen who were staying on the Loire. A great storm struck the *pagus* of Laon and Soissons, which blew down many trees and houses and killed many people in various places. William, the *princeps* of the Aquitanians, died.[58] The Northmen of the Loire were besieged for five weeks by Heribert and Hugh [the Great]. After hostages were offered and accepted and the *pagus* of Nantes was conceded to them, the Northmen agreed to a peace with the Franks.

[9C] A synod of six bishops was held at Trosly-Loire, but King Raoul prohibited the meeting through the envoys of Count Heribert and ordered Heribert to postpone the synod and to meet him at Compiègne. Heribert refused to do this and attended the synod. Count Erluinus [of Montreuil] came to the synod to do penance for marrying while his wife was still living. After the synod adjourned, Count Heribert wanted to enter Laon, but King

Raoul sent soldiers who prevented Heribert's guardianship of the place. King Raoul followed and entered the *castellum* [of Laon]. Heribert then freed [King] Charles from custody and took him to St-Quentin in the *pagus* of Vermandois. Raoul returned to Burgundy after leaving Laon in the hands of his wife [Emma] and the sons of Roger [count of Laon]. The sons then left the area around Coucy-le-Château, a *castrum* of the diocese of Reims, which they were devastating. [King] Charles and [Count] Heribert sought a meeting with the Northmen at the *castellum* of Eu, and there Rollo's son [William Longsword] committed himself to [King] Charles and affirmed his friendship with Heribert.[59] Fears resulting from a false rumor of [an invasion by] the Magyars led people to take flight throughout the Lotharingian kingdom and Francia.

10.

[10A] At the beginning of 928, during the period of the liturgies of the birth of Christ, [King] Raoul came from Burgundy with an invading force of Burgundians in order to plunder and burn certain places. Hugh [the Great], son of Robert, hurried to meet the king on the river Oise in the role of a mediator and a trustee between King Raoul and Count Heribert. Hugh took hostages from Heribert until they should meet again at a mutually agreeable *placitum*. Raoul then returned to Burgundy but was unable to persuade his wife [Emma] to leave Laon. Count Heribert came to Reims with [King] Charles and then sent a letter to Pope John [X] in Rome, informing him of the restoration and status (*honor*) of Charles and hoping that the pope might order [the Franks], under the threat of excommunication, to use their power on [King] Charles's behalf. King Raoul and Count Heribert met again at a *placitum* during Lent.[60] The queen, that is, Raoul's wife [Emma], gave up Laon and returned to Burgundy. Count Heribert then took possession of Laon and held a *placitum* with the Northmen, and he and Hugh [the Great], the son of Robert, made friendship with them. However, Odo, the son of Heribert [of Vermandois], whom Rollo was holding as a hostage, was not returned to his father until Heribert and certain other counts and bishops of Francia committed themselves to [King] Charles.

[10B] Different storms struck various places. Bishop Otgarius of Amiens died; he was a holy man and had lived to old age, being more than a hundred years old. Count Heribert [of Vermandois] took by storm the *munitio* of Mortagne-du-Nord on the river Scheldt, which belonged to the sons of Roger [of Laon], and destroyed it. In the meantime, the envoy of Count Heribert returned from Rome, bringing news that Pope John [X] had been imprisoned by Guy,[61] the brother of King Hugh [of Italy], because of a feud between the two. Bishop Odalricus of Aix-en-Provence was brought into the church of Reims by Count Heribert in order to perform the office of bishop on behalf of Hugh, Heribert's son, who was still only a boy.[62] [In compensation] the abbacy of St-Timothée[63] was conceded to Bishop Odalricus, along with a canon's prebend.

[10C] [King] Henry, the *princeps* of Germany, crossed the Rhine with a large force of Germans and arrived on the Meuse, where he besieged Count Boso's[64] *castrum* of Durofostum. This was because Boso was refusing to come to justice for certain abbeys and lands of the dioceses [of Verdun and Metz], which he had taken by the authority of his power and obstinately held despite Henry's commands. Henry sent a message to Boso, pledging peace to him if he should come to the king. After Boso received hostages from the king in a pact of security, he came to Henry and made an oath promising fidelity and peace to him within the kingdom. Boso then returned the lands that he had forcibly seized, receiving back in compensation various holdings. Then both Boso and Ragenarius were reconciled with Gislebert and the other Lotharingians.

[10D] Hugh [the Great] and Heribert [of Vermandois] set out for a conference with Henry [king of Germany]. After they returned, they continued on to meet with King Raoul. Again Heribert committed himself to Raoul and once again [King] Charles was put into custody. Finally, Heribert set out for Burgundy, along with Raoul, to meet Hugh, the king of Italy. The grape harvest was almost completed within the month of August. King Hugh [of Italy] had a conference with [King] Raoul and gave the province of Vienne to Count Heribert, in the place of Hugh's own son Odo. Bishop Benno of Metz was the victim of a plot and was castrated and blinded. King Raoul came to Reims and made peace with Charles, returning Attigny to him and honoring him with gifts.

II.

[11A] In the year 929, Count Heribert [of Vermandois] and Count Hugh [the Great] set out against [King] Raoul's brother Boso, who had seized certain allods of the recently deceased Rothildis,[65] Hugh's mother-in-law, which Hugh wanted back. Count Heribert took Boso's *castellum* of Vitry-en-Perthois and then both Hugh and Heribert granted Boso a truce to last until the end of the month of May. Boso went to [King] Henry and was compelled publicly to swear to peace.

[11B] Deroldus the physician (*medicus*) received the bishopric of Amiens and Adalbero received Metz, with Benno acquiring an abbey as a living. Heribert [of Vermandois] and Hugh [the Great] besieged the *castellum* of Montreuil, which belonged to Erluinus, the son of Count Hilgaudus [of Ponthieu]. After receiving hostages, they returned home.

[11C] Pope John [X] was deprived of his primacy (*principatus*) by Marozia,[66] a very powerful woman, and he was murdered while he was a captive. Some maintain that he was strangled.

[11D] King Charles died at Péronne.[67] A dispute arose between Count Hugh [the Great] and Count Heribert [of Vermandois] when Erluinus was received, along with his lands, by Hugh and when Hilduinus,[68] who was Hugh's man, was received by Heribert.

[11E] The Saracens blocked the Alpine paths and turned back many who wished to travel to Rome.

I2.

[12A] In the year 930, the Northmen of the Loire were attacking Aquitaine with plundering expeditions, but King Raoul almost annihilated them in a single battle in the *pagus* of Limoges. The king then made the Aquitanians submit themselves to him. Heribert [of Vermandois] received Arnold [count of Douai],[69] who had been the man of Hugh [the Great]. Hugh [the Great] and Heribert [of Vermandois] conducted various military operations against each other through Francia. King Raoul came into Francia and by great effort in a number of *placita* he made peace between Hugh, Heribert and [King Raoul's brother] Boso. Heribert then returned Vitry-en-Perthois to Boso. When Bishop Adelelmus of Laon died, he was succeeded by his nephew (*nepos*) Gosbert. Heribert received Ansellus, the vassal (*vassalus*)[70] of Boso, and the *castellum* of Vitry-en-Perthois that Ansellus was holding. Heribert then gave to Ansellus Coucy-le-Château and other lands.

[12B] When King Raoul returned to Burgundy, Gislebert and the Lotharingians came into Francia and met Hugh [the Great]. They besieged and captured the *oppidum* of Douai, which [Count] Arnold was holding. In the meantime Boso's men recaptured Vitry-en-Perthois through treachery and took Mouzon by a trick. Boso left some of his *fideles* as a garrison to guard Mouzon and himself set out to the siege of the aforesaid *castrum* [of Vitry]. However, Heribert [of Vermandois] was summoned by the inhabitants of Mouzon and he arrived there without being detected by crossing the Meuse by fords that he found. He entered the *oppidum* through a gate that the garrison (*castellani*) had secretly left open for him and captured all of Boso's vassals (*vassali*) whom he had left there to defend Mouzon.

[12C] At Reims, below and around the church of Saint Mary,[71] a great light appeared in the northern and eastern parts of the sky shortly before daybreak.

13.

[13A] In the year 931, King Raoul set out for Vienne to meet with Charles Constantine [the count of Vienne], the son of Louis the Blind, who was holding it. Charles Constantine promised to submit to Raoul and the king returned [to Burgundy]. He then set out for Tours to pray at [the monastery of] Saint Martin. In the meantime, the Lotharingians captured Douai and Hugh [the Great] conceded it to Roger, the son of Roger [of Laon]. Indeed, in return Heribert [of Vermandois] restored the *castrum* of St-Quentin to Arnold [of Douai].

[13B] The Greeks pursued the Saracens over the sea and all the way to the mountain pass of Freinet, which was their refuge and from which they made terrible raids on Italy and even occupied the Alps. But with God's help the Greeks swiftly routed and slaughtered the Saracens and returned from the Alps to an Italy at peace.

[13C] On the day of the Purification of Mary [2 February], the blessed mother of God, at her church in Reims,[72] a servant (*famulus*) of the canons, who was the custodian of the church of Sts. Denis and Tedulfus, was suddenly struck with paralysis. The tendons of his hands and feet contracted and he fell down, with his mouth seeming to stick to the stone of the pavement. A little later he was lifted up, but his hands and feet were drawn up with paralysis and he was carried out, unable to move. Shortly afterwards, on a Sunday [6 February], the fifth day after this happened, suddenly his hands could move, and then at mass his legs [could also move], which was on the fifteenth day. A similar thing had happened to him five years earlier, on the day of the Circumcision of the Lord [1 January 926], in the same church. And he was able to move again thirty days later, on the solemnity of the Purification [2 February].

[13D] Bishop Robert [II] of Tours was returning from Rome and while in the Alps he and his companions were killed in their tents at night by brigands.

[13E] Gislebert,[73] the son of Manasses, withdrew his allegiance from King Raoul because Queen Emma had taken away from him the *castrum* of Avallon. Likewise Richard,[74] the son of Warnerius, defected for the same reason. Similarly, a conflict arose between Gislebert the Lotharingian and Boso [the brother of King Raoul], and Boso made a peace pact with Heribert [of Vermandois]. Boso's *castrum* of Durofostum was captured by Gislebert, and at the same time the *munitio* of Mortagne-du-Nord, which belonged to the sons of Roger [of Laon], was taken by Arnulf, Baldwin's son.[75] Heribert accepted the friendship of Gislebert the Lotharingian. Boso, having renounced his allegiance to Henry [king of Germany], went to King Raoul. Boso then returned to the *castrum* of Châlons-sur-Marne and captured it by force. He then set it on fire and destroyed it. This was due to the hostility of Bishop Bovo of Châlons, whose men had lopped off limbs of some of Boso's men. King Raoul returned to Francia. Because Count Heribert had deserted from him, the king and Hugh [the Great] captured and destroyed Heribert's *castellum* of Denain. Next the king besieged Arras. Count Heribert, who was joined by the Lotharingians due to the efforts of Duke Gislebert, advanced against the king. However, both sides departed after agreeing to a truce that was to last until the first day of October.

[13F] Meanwhile, some of Heribert's *fideles* left the *urbs* of Reims and captured and destroyed the *castrum* of Braisne, on the river Vesle. Earlier, Hugh [the Great] had taken this place from [Gontard] the [arch]bishop of Rouen. King Raoul sent a letter to the clergy and people of Reims for them to have an election of a bishop. They answered the king that they could not do this, for they had already chosen a bishop who was well and their election stood. Count Heribert went to Henry [king of Germany] and committed himself to him. An army of King [Raoul] and of Hugh [the Great] pillaged Laon and the *pagus* of Reims. King Raoul proceeded on to Attigny and sent Hugh to [King] Henry, and [King] Henry returned across the Rhine after receiving hostages and a pact of security from Hugh.

[13G] In the meantime, on the solemnities of Saint Michael [29 September] the Bretons who had remained subdued by the Northmen in Cournouaille rose up against those who were holding them in their power. It was said that they killed all the Northmen who were found among them, and the first who died was their commander (*dux*), Felecan.

[13H] King Raoul and Hugh [the Great], Boso and other of his men besieged the *urbs* of Reims. After the siege had lasted for three weeks, those who were in the *civitas* opened it to the besiegers.[76] Raoul entered the city and had ordained as bishop there Artoldus, a monk from the monastery of St-Rémi who earlier in this year had deserted Heribert and gone over to Hugh. The king also captured Bishop Bovo of Châlons, who had deserted from Raoul along with Heribert. He placed Bovo into Hugh's custody and handed the bishopric of Châlons over to the cleric Milo. The king continued on to Laon and laid siege to Heribert, who had immured himself and his men there. Heribert did not hold out for very long but was allowed to leave Laon after despatching his wife[77] to hold the citadel that he had constructed inside the city. King Raoul was able to take the citadel after immense effort and considerable delay. After this, Raoul returned to Burgundy and set out to meet the rebellious Aquitanians. The Northman Incon, who was staying on the Loire, invaded Brittany with his men. He gained possession of the region after defeating, plundering, killing and expelling the Bretons.

14.

[14A] In the year 932, King Raoul returned to Burgundy and recaptured some *castella* that belonged to Gislebert and Richard,[78] who had deserted him. Bishop Airardus of Noyon died and one of the clerics of this *urbs* who wanted to become bishop allowed Count Adelelmus [of Arras] to climb the wall of the *civitas* in secret at night. In the morning the count drove out the soldiers from the *urbs*, but they collected some men from the suburbs and attacked the *civitas*. Those inside the walls counterattacked, nonetheless some entered by a burned gate and others through a church window. Adelelmus fled into the church and was killed next to the altar along with others who had entered with him. Thus the townsmen (*cives*) of Noyon regained the *urbs*.

[14B] After Count Heribert [of Vermandois] received the surrender of the *castrum* of Ham, he captured Ebrardus, the brother of Erluinus [the count of Montreuil and Ponthieu], who had been holding it. King Raoul conferred with Hugh [the Great] and received Bishop Bovo into his favor and returned to him the bishopric of Châlons. Abbot Waltbert of Corbie was ordained bishop of Noyon. King Raoul received Gislebert [of Chalon] and left Burgundy for Francia, where he gained possession of the abbey of St-Médard [of Soissons], previously held by Heribert [of Vermandois], and then he returned to Burgundy.

[14C] Hugh [the Great] and some of the bishops of Francia laid siege to the *civitas* of Amiens, which was being held by Heribert's *fideles*. He attacked repeatedly and finally withdrew when many hostages had been offered to him. He then moved on to surround the *castrum* of St-Quentin and place it under siege. Milo[79] pillaged the diocese of Châlons and was excommunicated by Archbishop Artoldus [of Reims] and the other bishops of the province of Reims. After a siege of two months Hugh captured the *castellum* of St-Quentin when the garrison (*oppidani*) surrendered. On the day after he entered St-Quentin, a man who had been crippled was cured in the church.

[14D] [The count of Toulouse,] Raymond[-Pons III] and Ermingaudus [count of Rouergue], *principes* of Gothia, committed themselves to King Raoul, as did Lupus Acinarius the Gascon, who was said to have a horse that was more than a hundred years old yet was still very strong. [Duke] Gislebert, at the the invitation of Hugh [the Great], besieged Péronne[80] with the Lotharingians. Many Lotharingians died in the frequent encounters and the remaining Lotharingians, unable to take the *munitio*, withdrew after Hugh mediated a conference between Duke Gislebert and King Raoul. King Raoul and Hugh [the Great] placed under siege Heribert's *castellum* of Ham. After receiving hostages they raised the siege. Bishop Gosbert of Laon died, and Ingoramnus, the dean[81] of the monastery of St-Médard [of Soissons] was ordained bishop of Laon. Boso, the king's brother, and Bishop Bernuinus of

Verdun made an orgy (*bacchantur*) with fires and raids. Heribert [of Vermandois] set out across the Rhine to Henry [king of Germany].

15.

[15A] In the year 933, Giso and Amalricus, envoys of the church of Reims, returned from Rome and brought the *pallium* to [Arch]bishop Artoldus. They reported that Pope John [XI], the son of Mary, also called Marozia, was held in custody by his brother Alberic. Alberic also kept his mother Marozia under confinement and held Rome against King Hugh [of Italy].[82] The Magyars divided their forces into three units. One of them went to Italy and another invaded the lands of Henry [king of Germany] across the Rhine. Henry set out against them, along with the Bavarians and Saxons and other peoples who were subject to him. He cut down all of them, almost exterminating them. It is said that 36,000 were killed, not including those who drowned in the river or those taken alive.[83]

[15B] Richarius, the bishop of Tongres, demolished a *castellum* of Count Bernard,[84] which the count had built at Charleville in the *pagus* of Porcien. This was because it was located on lands belonging to his church. The men who held Vienne handed it over to King Raoul. William [Longsword], the *princeps* of the Northmen, committed himself to the king [Raoul], who then gave William the land of the Bretons that was located along the sea coast.[85] For six weeks King Raoul besieged Château-Thierry, a *munitio* of Heribert. Afterwards, Walo, who had held it, committed himself to Queen Emma and the *castrum* was given to her faith and care.

[15C] Bishop Waldricus of Auxerre died and Guy, the archdeacon of Auxerre, obtained the bishopric. A synod was held [at Reims] during the aforesaid siege [of Château-Thierry]. Many bishops of Francia and Burgundy attended, with Lord Artoldus, the [arch]bishop of Reims, and Lord Teotolo, [arch]bishop of Tours, presiding. At that synod Lord Artoldus also ordained Hildegarius as bishop of the *urbs* of Beauvais.

[15D] Heribert [of Vermandois]'s son Odo, who was holding the *praesidium* of Ham, raided throughout the *pagus* of Soissons and Noyon, looting and burning as he went. His father Heribert came in secret to St-Quentin and on the third day took the *castrum* by fighting. The residents of the place (*oppidani*) did not put up a resistance, but only the garrison (*custodes*) placed there by Hugh [the Great]. Heribert captured the garrison and then released them after they gave him oaths [not to fight again]. He then left his own supporters there to hold the *oppidum*. When Hugh [the Great] heard what had happened, he came quickly to St-Quentin and took it. He captured a certain noble cleric named Treduinus, who had been sent there by Heribert, and hanged him along with others. He also mutilated many others by cutting off various limbs.

He then set out with Lord [Arch]bishop Artoldus and easily captured the *munitio* of Roye when Heribert's garrison handed it over to him.

[15E] King Hugh of Italy besieged Rome, and the Saracens occupied the Alpine passes, plundering all the surrounding area. Archbishop Artoldus ordained Fulbert as bishop of the *urbs* of Cambrai. Heribert [of Vermandois] received Château-Thierry, located on the Marne, when the garrison that Walo had left there handed it over. Heribert put his own men there to guard it and departed. When Hugh [the Great] heard this, he carefully laid siege to the same *castrum* as quickly as possible.

16.

[16A] In the year 934, King Raoul and Count Hugh [the Great] laid siege to the aforesaid *munitio* [of Château-Thierry]. In the fourth month of the siege, at night when the garrison (*custodes*) was sleeping, Walo and his men climbed the walls and captured a part of the *oppidum*. However, the better prepared citadel was still held by Heribert's *fideles*. Not long after this, at the urging of the royal soldiers, they gave hostages and Walo broke off the siege.

[16B] At Reims, in the church of Mary the Blessed Mother of God,[86] on the feast of the Annunciation of the Lord [25 March], [Arch]bishop Artoldus was celebrating masses there. Then a certain young man, who was accustomed to crawl because the tendons of his knees were drawn up, suddenly stood up as his joints were loosened and his legs straightened out, and he walked again on the feet that had been forgotten for so long. Likewise, in the church of Saint Hilary, which is located [in Reims] just inside the gate of Mars,[87] a blind man named Paul regained his sight. Earlier he had been told in a dream that he would receive his sight there.

[16C] King Raoul and Hugh [the Great] resumed the siege [of Château-Thierry], when the hostages that they had given Heribert [of Vermandois] had been neglected.

[16D] Henry [king of Germany] sent [Duke] Gislebert [of Lotharingia] and [Count] Ebrardus [of Franconia], along with the bishops of Lothair's Kingdom, to King Raoul on behalf of Heribert. Château-Thierry was returned to the king and Ham and Péronne were conceded to Heribert until 1 October. Arnulf [I, the Old] of Flanders took as his wife Heribert's daughter [Adele], to whom he had already been betrothed through an exchange of oaths. Heribert gathered the harvests throughout the *pagus* of Vermandois from those who had abandoned the land that Hugh [the Great] had given them, which he had taken to Péronne.

[16E] At Reims, just before the break of day on 14 October, a line of fire was seen in the sky running in different directions, just like a serpent of fire, and iron javelins were also seen in the sky. A plague followed soon after this, afflicting humans with various ailments. Adelmarus, a deacon of Verdun, fell ill and was seen to have let go of his spirit. However, before he was placed on a bier, he returned and rose so healthy that no trace of the illness remained. He testified that he had seen various places of prayer and of refreshment, and he was condemned to a place of punishment. But by the prayers of the Mother of God and by the intercession of Blessed Martin, he had been returned to his present life in order to do penance.

[16F] [Duke] Gislebert and the Lotharingians came into Francia to assist Heribert [of Vermandois], who was about to besiege the *oppidum* of St-Quentin. However, before he had reached it, envoys of Hugh [the Great] came and met with him, and when oaths were given on both sides, they made peace between Hugh [the Great] and Heribert [of Vermandois] that was to last until the month of May. The Lotharingians then returned home.

[16G] The religion of the rule of monks[88] was restored in certain monasteries throughout Lothair's Kingdom. Queen Emma died.

Fig. 2. Mars Gate, Reims

The largest triumphal arch known to have been built in the Roman Empire.

From *Reims and the Battles for its Possession* (Clermont-Ferrand: Michelin & Cie, 1919) 82.

17.

[17A] In the year 935, King Raoul besieged and captured the *castrum* of Vitry, which belonged to Geoffrey [count of Nevers] and which certain Aquitainians were holding against him. The king then returned it to Geoffrey and moved into Francia, sending Geoffrey across the Rhine to meet with Henry [king of Germany]. On the holy day of Easter [29 March], while King Raoul was residing at Laon, there was a clash between the king's soldiers and those of the bishop [Ingoramnus], during which many of the laity as well as clergy were wounded or killed. After this, the king held a *placitum* at Soissons with the magnates (*primates*) of the kingdom. Afterwards, the king spoke with Henry's envoys and hurried to a meeting with him, where Rudolf [II], the king of the Jura [Upper Burgundy], was also present. A pact of friendship was made between them and they even arranged a reconciliation between Heribert and Hugh, with certain of Heribert's possessions being returned to him. [King] Henry received Boso and restored to him most of the land that he had previously held [in the Lotharingian kingdom].

[17B] The Magyars attacked throughout Burgundy, raging with plunderings, fires and murder. However, this raiding lasted for only a short time, for when the Magyars learned of King Raoul's coming, they moved on into Italy. Archbishop Artoldus [of Reims] ordained the monk Wicfredus as bishop of the church of Thérouanne.

[17C] King Raoul besieged the *castrum* of Dijon, which Count Boso [brother of King Raoul] had captured and which his accomplices were holding. The Lotharingians, along with some counts from Saxony who were Heribert's friends, along with a large army, came to a kind of meeting with Hugh [the Great]. But because Hugh refused to return the *castellum* of St-Quentin to Heribert, they besieged that *munitio*, which they attacked vigorously and, when the garrison (*tutantes*) surrendered, they captured it. They then made the fortifications indefensible. They were preparing to besiege Laon but returned into their own lands at the command of King Raoul.

[17D] In the meantime King Raoul's brother Boso died on an expedition to besiege the *castrum* of St-Quentin. He was taken to [the monastery of] St-Rémi and buried there. King Raoul lay seriously ill throughout the entire autumn. The Northmen who had plundered the *pagus* of Bourges were destroyed in battle by the men of Berry and the Touraine. Lord Archbishop Artoldus presided over a synod of seven bishops at Ste-Macre. At this synod those who had robbed and besieged the lands of the church were summoned to correct their deeds.

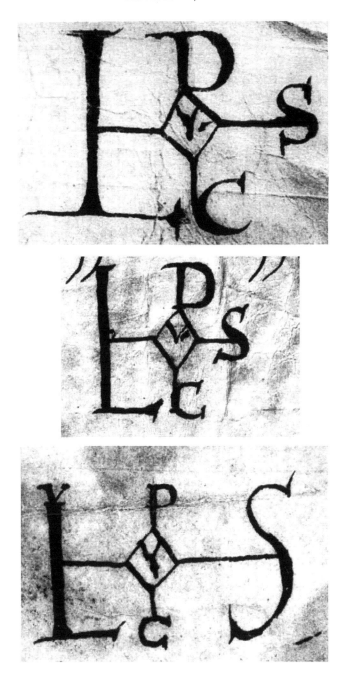

Fig. 3. Monograms of King Louis IV ("Ludovicus")

From *Recueil des Actes de Louis IV, roi de France (936-954)*, ed. Maurice Prou and Philippe Lauer (Paris: C. Klincksieck, 1914) pl. 5.

18.

[18A] In the year 936, Ingramnus, the bishop of the church of Laon, died. On almost the same day King Raoul died and was buried at the church of Saint Columba at Sens,[89] which had been burned by a faction of men a little before. The Bretons from across the sea, with the support of King Aethelstan [of the English], returned and took back their land.[90] Count Hugh [the Great] sent across the sea [to England] and summoned Louis, the son of Charles [the Simple], to take up the rule of the kingdom [of Francia]. Louis's uncle, King Aethelstan, sent him to Francia along with bishops and others of his *fideles* after oaths had been given by the legates of the Franks. Hugh and the rest of the nobles (*proceres*) of the Franks set out to meet Louis when he left the ship, and they committed themselves to him on the beach at Boulogne-sur-Mer just as both sides had previously agreed. They then conducted Louis to Laon and he was consecrated king, anointed and crowned by Lord Archbishop Artoldus [of Reims], in the presence of the *principes* of the kingdom and more than twenty bishops.

[18B] The bishopric of Laon was given to the priest Raoul, who was from Laon, following his peaceful election by the townsmen (*cives*). He was consecrated as bishop by Lord [Archbishop] Artoldus.[91] The king and Hugh [the Great] proceeded into Burgundy and laid siege to the *urbs* of Langres, which had been seized by Hugh [the Black], King Raoul's brother. Louis and Hugh took the city without fighting when the garrison fled. They then went to Paris after they received hostages from the bishops and the magnates (*primates*) of Burgundy. Because King Henry [of Germany] had died during that time [2 July 936], there arose a conflict over the kingdom among his sons, with the highest position falling to his son Otto, being better by birth.[92]

[18C] On 4 September, the fourteen-day-old moon [full moon] was covered in the color of blood and scarcely seemed to light up the night.[93] Pope John [XI], brother of the patrician Alberic, died and Leo [VII], a servant of God, was established as pope in Rome.[94] King Hugh of Italy exerted himself to take Rome, but his army was afflicted by a famine and by the loss of its horses. Hugh then made peace with Alberic, giving him his own daughter [Alda] as a wife, and he broke off the siege. But when he learned of some plots against him by the men of his brother Boso, it is said, he captured his brother by a trick and kept him under guard.

[18D] The Saracens raided Alamannia and, as they were returning, they killed many who were traveling to Rome. Hugh [the Great], the son of Robert, made peace with Hugh [the Black], the son of Richard [the Justiciar], and they divided Burgundy between themselves.[95] Bishop Adelelmus of Senlis died.

19.

[19A] In the year 937, Bernuinus, who was from the monastery of St-Crépin [of Soissons], was ordained bishop of Senlis. Bishop Waltbert of Noyon also died and was succeeded by Transmarus, the prior of the monastery of Saint Vaast [of Arras].

[19B] King Louis withdrew himself from the management of the *princeps* Hugh [the Great][96] and received his mother [Eadgifu] at Laon. Hugh made peace with Heribert [of Vermandois], who received the *castellum* of Château-Thierry when Walo opened it to him. Walo became Heribert's man but then Heribert threw him into chains.

[19C] A part of the sky seemed to be burning and afterwards there was an invasion of Francia by the Magyars from that direction, with *villae* and fields laid waste, houses and basilicas burned, and large number of captives led away. However, although they tried to set fire to many other churches they were not able to do so. They were unable to set fire to the church of Ste-Macre [at Fismes] even though they placed two burning stacks of hay against it. In the church of St-Basle, one of the Magyars tried to climb on the altar, placing his hand on it. But his hand stuck to the stone of the altar and he was not able to free his hand by any means. Finally, other Magyars chipped the stone away around his hand [to which it was still attached], which the pagan (*ethnicus*) displayed to the astonishment of the others.

[19D] Adalgarius, a priest of the church of the *villa* of Bouvaincourt, was captured by the Magyars and taken away into the *pagus* of Berry. As he was in chains and leg irons, a vision appeared to a woman, a fellow captive, who was ordered to tell the priest that he should escape when he should see that he had been released from his bonds. Just as it was shown in the vision, his shackles were opened. But the priest feared that the barbarian might kill him, as he had often threatened to do if the priest should be captured trying to escape. So the priest, not daring to escape, placed the chains back around his feet, placing back into position the bolt on the chains. On the next night the same vision came to the same female captive, who encouraged the priest to take flight, and again his chains were loosened. At last, the priest made his escape and lay in a marsh for a few days until he learned that the barbarians had left. He then returned to his own fatherland and related to us what he, as a captive, had seen concerning Hucbaldus, a monk of the monastery of Orbais[-l'Abbaye]. The pagans tried to kill him many times, but they were unable to cut into his flesh. Therefore they said that he was a god. The priest reported that a certain man saw Hucbaldus standing naked in the middle of crowd that was shooting arrows at him from all sides but his skin was not penetrated at all. The arrows simply bounced off his body as if from steel without leaving any trace of a wound on his skin. The man also saw the defenseless Hucbaldus being attacked with a sword that was being wielded vigorously, yet his flesh remained unharmed.

[19E] After a long exile, The Bretons returned to their places and fought many battles against the Northmen, who had invaded that land which was next to their own. The Bretons won many of the encounters and took over the places that the Northman had invaded. Rudolf [II], the king of Jurane and Cisalpine Gaul,[97] died and he was succeeded by his young son Conrad.[98]

[19F] Bishop Abbo of Soissons died and Guy, the son of [Count] Fulk [the Red] of Anjou, a canon of St-Martin of Tours, gained his diocese.

20.

[20A] In the year 938, King Louis took by force the *castrum* of Montigny-Lengrain, which Serlus, who had been acting as a brigand, had been holding. King Louis spared the life of Serlus at the request of Archbishop Artoldus [of Reims], but he destroyed the *oppidum*. Louis received Heribert [of Vermandois] in peace at the request of Hugh [the Great]. Louis's father [King Charles the Simple] had given Tusey on the Meuse and other *villae* pertaining to it to Louis's mother [Eadgifu] as a dowry, but Count Roger[99] came to hold them. King Louis set out to regain them by military force and was successful. Returning from there, the king captured the *castellum* of Corbeny, which his father had handed over to [the monastery of] St-Rémi [at Reims] and which Heribert [of Vermandois] had invaded. The king captured by force what had been committed to him by the monks and, at the request of Lord Archbishop Artoldus [of Reims], he allowed Heribert's men who were in it to depart. The *princeps* Hugh [the Great], son of Robert, married [Hadwig] the sister of Otto, the Transrhenine king, and thus the daughter of [King] Henry. King Louis went to the sea coast and worked to restore the *castrum* and *portus* of Guines. While he delayed there with Arnulf [count of Flanders], Heribert's men captured the *castrum* of Chausot, on the Marne, which belonged to the church of Reims and which had been constructed by [Arch]bishop Artoldus. Wipertus betrayed the place and Heribert's men took as their prisoner Ragebertus,[100] the commander of the *castrum*, whom they led away with them as they plundered the *villae* of the area with frequent raids.

[20B] Meanwhile, King Louis had been summoned [to Reims] by Archbishop Artoldus and then returned and entered Laon, laying siege to the new citadel that Heribert [of Vermandois] had built. The wall was undermined and broken by many machines and the citadel was taken by great effort. Then the king set out to meet with Hugh [the Black, duke of Burgundy], the brother of the late king Raoul, leaving the defense of Laon to Odo, son of Heribert, who had just committed himself to Louis. Hugh [the Black] came to the king and made an oath promising friendship to Louis. [Duke] Gislebert and the Lotharingians came to Hugh [the Great] and Heribert to assist them against King Louis, and they captured by force the *castrum* of Pierrepont. Count Arnulf [of Flanders] and Heribert agreed to an adjournment with King Louis and Hugh [the Black] and by an oath they arranged a peace to last until the end of the month of January. King Louis took the counsel of Odoinus and Gerardus, who had abandoned Bishop Raoul [II] of Laon and had gone over to Hugh [the Great], and without delay the king plundered and dispersed the treasures found in Laon.

21.

[21A] In the year 939, King Louis set out to meet Hugh [the Black], son of Richard, and returned with him from Burgundy. He then attacked Hugh [the Great], son of Robert, and William [Longsword], the *princeps* of the Northmen. William had been excommunicated by the bishops who had been with the king because he had recently ravaged with raids and fire some *villae* belonging to Count Arnulf [of Flanders]. Heribert [of Vermandois] had also been excommunicated for obstinately holding certain *oppida* and for usurping *villae* of [the monastery of] St-Rémi. Hugh gave hostages to the king and made a peace with him that was to last until the first day of June.

[21B] The Lotharingians deserted their king Otto and came to King Louis, who delayed receiving them because of the firm friendship between the two kings, which had been arranged by legates of this Otto [I, king of Germany] and of Count Arnulf [of Flanders]. Count Arnulf captured the coastal *castellum* of Montreuil, which belonged to Erluinus [count of Montreuil and Ponthieu], when a traitor handed it over to him. Arnulf [captured] Erluinus's wife and children and sent them across the sea to King Aethelstan [of the English].[101] Not long afterwards, Erluinus, aided by a large force of Northmen, recaptured the *castrum* by force. He killed some of Arnulf's soldiers whom he found inside, but he spared the lives of others [in order to exchange them] so that he might regain his wife.

[21C] Likewise the Lotharingians came to King Louis and the magnates (*proceres*) of the Lotharingian kingdom, namely Duke Gislebert and the counts Otho [of Verdun], Isaac [of Cambrai] and Theoderic [of Holland], and committed themselves to Louis. However, the bishops delayed committing themselves to King Louis because King Otto was holding their hostages with him. King Otto crossed the Rhine and passed through the Lotharingian kingdom, devastating many places by fire and pillaging.

[21D] The fleet of the English was sent by their king Aethelstan to assist King Louis, but when they crossed the sea, they plundered the coast of Flanders.[102] Without accomplishing anything of their original mission, they went back across the sea from where they had come. King Otto held a meeting with Hugh [the Great], Heribert [of Vermandois], Arnulf [of Flanders] and William, the *princeps* of the Northmen. He made a pact with them that was supported by an oath and then returned across the Rhine.

[21E] Meanwhile, King Louis set out for the *pagus* of Verdun where some bishops of Lothair's Kingdom became his men. From there he left for the *pagus* of Alsace and spoke with the Cisalpine Hugh [the Black]. He also received some Lotharingians who came to meet him. Among these were many of King Otto's *fideles* who were fleeing across the Rhine. In addition, he evicted Bishop Raoul [II] of Laon, who was accused of treachery, from the *castrum* [of Laon] and he deprived the bishop's men of the the properties of this diocese and gave them to his own men.

[21F] Duke Gislebert of the Lotharingians set out raiding across the Rhine and was returning with the Saxons in pursuit. He jumped into the Rhine with his horse and was killed by the force of the water. His body was never found but it is said that fishermen discovered the corpse of a man, which was buried and concealed because of his equipment.

[21G] King Louis returned to the Lotharingian kingdom and married Gerberga, the widow of Gislebert, that is, the sister of King Otto. A group of people from various places who were journeying to Rome were seized and killed by Saracens. The Bretons fought against the Northmen and gained the victory. It was said that they captured a certain *castellum* of the Northmen.[103] Some men of Arnulf [of Flanders] plundered the lands of Erluinus [count of Montreuil and Ponthieu], who killed them. King Otto returned into the Lotharingian kingdom and forced almost all of the Lotharingians to return to him. Hugh the White[104] [the Great] set out to his meeting with Heribert [of Vermandois], and as they returned they plundered some places of the *fideles* of the church of Reims, many of which they then burned.

22.

[22A] In the year 940, King Louis went to a meeting with William [Longsword], the *princeps* of the Northmen, who met him in the *pagus* of Amiens and committed himself to the king. Louis gave William the land that his father [King] Charles had conceded to the Northmen and then set out against Hugh [the Great]. But when Hugh refused to meet him, Louis returned to Laon. However, the king, through a written royal order, gave in perpetuity to Archbishop Artoldus and thus to the church of Reims the mint of the *urbs* of Reims. But he conferred the entire county of Reims to the same church.[105] Archbishop Artoldus then laid siege to the *munitio* of Chausot and on the fifth day, after King Louis had arrived there, the defenders surrendered and deserted. A short time later the place was undermined and thus completely destroyed by those who had taken it.

[22B] Envoys sent by Hugh [the Great] came to King Louis, who was eager to establish peace between them on one side and [Arch]bishop Artoldus [of Reims] and Heribert [of Vermandois] on the other. The king then set out with Bishop Artoldus to the *castrum* on the Marne [Châtillon-sur-Marne], which Heriveus, the nephew (*nepos*) of the former bishop Heriveus, was holding. From that place he had been pillaging nearby *villae* belonging to the diocese of Reims. The king quickly returned to Reims after receiving hostages from this Heriveus. On the next day, he went to [the monastery of] St-Rémi and committed himself to the intercessions of the saint, promising that he would give a pound of silver every year for the fording of the river. He also gave to the monks of St-Rémi a precept of immunity[106] for the same *castellum*.

[22C] The *princeps* Hugh [the Great], Robert's son, when certain bishops of both Francia and Burgundy had joined with him, besieged the *urbs* of Reims, along with Count Heribert [of Vermandois] and William [Longsword], the *princeps* of the Northmen. On the sixth day of the siege, when almost the entire force of soldiers deserted Archbishop Artoldus and joined Heribert, this same Heribert entered the *urbs*. Bishop Artoldus, who had set out to [the monastery of] St-Rémi at the summons of the magnates (*proceres*) and bishops, was terrified by the *principes* [Heribert and William] and was persuaded to abdicate from the office and power of his see. The *abbatia* of St-Basle was conceded to him and he withdrew to the monastery of Avenay, to stay at St-Basle.[107] Hugh and Heribert spoke with certain Lotharingians and set out with William to lay siege to Laon. The deacon Hugh, Heribert's son, who had been called to the episcopacy of this *urbs* a long time before[108] was left behind at Reims [as bishop].[109]

[22D] After staying in Burgundy for six or seven weeks, King Louis returned, bringing with him Archbishop Artoldus with his kinsmen, as well as his companions, whose benefices (*beneficia*) Count Heribert [of Vermandois] had stolen. The king came to the Champagne *pagus* of Reims, and when he had crossed the river Aisne he advanced on Laon. When Hugh [the Great] and Heribert learned of this, they gave up the siege of Laon and hurried by night to the *munitio* of Pierrepont, and [from there] they set out to meet King Otto [of Germany]. After joining him, they conducted him to Attigny and there they, along with Count Roger [of Laon], committed themselves to [King] Otto.

[22E] King Louis entered Laon and provided his men with necessary sustenance. Then, along with Hugh the Black [duke of Burgundy] and William [Towhead, count] of Poitou, he returned to Burgundy. King Otto gave [the administration of] the Lotharingian kingdom to his brother Henry [duke of Bavaria]. Then, with a multitude of diverse peoples whom he had gathered with him, Otto set out into Burgundy after King Louis. Otto had with him

[King] Conrad [III of Upper Burgundy], son of King Rudolf [II] of Jura, whom he had captured by means of a ruse and whom he kept with him. Otto laid out his fortified encampment on the banks of the Seine and received hostages from Hugh the Black, who also swore that he would not harm Hugh [the Great] or Heribert [of Vermandois], who had committed themselves to Otto. When this was completed, Otto returned home. Hugh, son of Heribert [of Vermandois], was ordained priest at Reims by Bishop Guy of Soissons. King Louis returned to Laon.

[22F] Finally, I decided to visit the tomb of Saint Martin [at Tours] so that I might pray there. However, I was detained by Count Heribert [of Vermandois] when some men had made secret accusations against me, that I wanted to set out in order to harm him or his son, and he had me held in custody. He also took from me the things that I was holding from the diocese, along with the church in Cormicy that I administered. Thus I was held in custody for five full months.[110] King Louis attacked the *munitio* of Pierrepont, withdrawing from it after he had received hostages. He then set out into the Lotharingian kingdom with Archbishop Artoldus [of Reims] and with others of his *fideles*. King Otto crossed the Rhine and came out against him. However, a truce was arranged between them by their *fideles*.

[22G] A girl named Flotildis, a poor maiden from the *villa* of Lavannes, was eagerly looking for visions of the saints and was accustomed to see in the spirit and predict the future. In the next year, she died on the night of the Lord's birth.

[22H] In this year, on a Sunday night in the month of December, a line of various colors was seen in the sky. A group of people from across the sea and from Gaul were returning from Rome, and the Saracens prevented them from crossing the Alps, killing many of them. The Saracens had occupied the *vicus* of the monastery of St-Maurice-en-Valais.[111]

23.

[23A] In the year 941, Gerlandus, the archbishop of Sens, was driven from his *urbs* by Frotmundus [viscount of Sens], whom Hugh the White [the Great] had put in charge of the same *civitas*. Gerlandus was blamed for this because he supported Walo, Count Heribert's man, who had expelled Frotumundus and his men from the *urbs* of Sens.

[23B] Count Heribert [of Vermandois] called a synod to settle the dispute [over the archbishopric of Reims] between his son Hugh and Archbishop Artoldus. However, Hugh [the Great] obstructed the process and was active to stop it lest those who would attend it should do so for the fidelity and aid of King Louis, and the synod did not meet.

[23C] King Louis set out for Burgundy and learned that Count Roger [of Laon] had by chance laid out his camp close to his own. The king went to the river Marne and captured Count Roger, along with those who were with him, and led them with him into Burgundy.

[23D] The counts Hugh [the Great] and Heribert [of Vermandois] summoned the bishops of the province of Reims, who then met together at Soissons, in the church of Saints Crispin and Crispinianus. They dealt with the status of the diocese of Reims and resolved to do something about it. Clerics and nobles of the laity complained that this see had lacked a pastor for a long time and, because [Arch]bishop Artoldus [of Reims] had sworn that he had never meddled in that diocese, it ought to be returned to the administration of Hugh, the son of Count Heribert. Indeed, Hugh, who earlier had been called to this bishopric, was ordained bishop at the request of both clergy and laity. The first thing that this Hugh did was to command that I be recalled from exile. The bishops then went to Reims so that Hugh, our bishop-elect, could be consecrated bishop at [the monastery of] St-Rémi [at Reims].

[23E] After Count Roger [of Laon] gave hostages, he was set free by King Louis and the *castellum* of Douai was returned to [Count] Arnold [of Douai].[112] The monastery of St-Thierry became famous due to its divine miracles. The large cross of the church of Reims,[113] adorned with wrought gold and precious gems, was secretly stolen from the same church. The canons of Montfaucon, burdened by the oppression of the bishop of Verdun [Berengar], deserted their monastery and carried the body of Saint Baldericus, their patron, to Reims.

[23F] King Louis set out for Burgundy and made peace between Count Roger [of Laon] on one side and Hugh the Black and [Count] Gislebert[114] on the other. The king then stayed at Laon and drove Arnold [of Douai] and his brother Landricus, both of whom having been accused of treachery, from Laon's *castrum*. The king gave the county of Laon to Roger. When King Louis learned that Hugh the White [the Great] had hurried to besiege Laon, Louis again set out for the parts of Burgundy with [Arch]bishop Artoldus and Count Roger. When Louis delayed around the *castrum* of Vitry-en-Perthois [or le Brûlé], Hugh [the Great] and Heribert [of Vermandois] laid siege to Laon. However, the king came into the *pagus* of Porcien with the men whom he was able to collect from anywhere he could. When Hugh and Heribert learned that the king was coming against them, they raised the siege and hurried out against the king, catching Louis's army by surprise and killing many, while others fled. The king and a few others were barely able to escape. Louis was led away by his own men who forced him to give up the battle. [Arch]bishop Artoldus and Count Roger [of Laon] accompanied the king in flight. [Arch]bishop Artoldus, who had now lost everything, came to Hugh and

Heribert and gave them the oaths that they required, and they returned to him the abbeys of St-Basle and Avenay, with the *villa* of Vendress. After [Archbishop] Artoldus made peace with [Arch]bishop Hugh [of Reims], he took up his residence at St-Basle. Hugh and Heribert abandoned the siege of Laon. A son [Lothair] was born to King Louis. The aforesaid counts spoke with William [Longsword]¹¹⁵ and wanted to resume the siege of Laon soon, having made an agreement that the *castrum* of Laon would be surrendered to them by treachery. But when this did not come about, they returned home. King Louis was received in Vienne by Charles Constantine [count of Vienne]. The Aquitainians came to him and acknowledged him [as king]. Hugh [the Great], Heribert [of Vermandois], William [Longsword] and Arnulf [of Flanders] met together, and Heribert then set out across the Rhine to go to King Otto.

24.

[24A] In the year 942, after the Aquitainians were allied to him, King Louis returned to Laon. However, he did not remain there for a long time, for there was no peace, and he went to Burgundy. Damasus, the legate of Pope Stephen [IX], was ordained bishop at Rome for the purpose of fulfilling this mission and came to Francia, carrying a letter of the apostolic see to the *principes* of the kingdom and to all the inhabitants of Francia and Burgundy so that they might receive Louis as their king. However, if they should fail to do this and should continue to attack him with a hostile sword, the pope would excommunicate them. Therefore the bishops of the province of Reims spoke with Count Heribert [of Vermandois] and begged him to interecede with the *princeps* Hugh [the Great] to accept the king.

[24B] Some traitors were discovered at Reims and were killed. Others were deprived of the resources that they held from the church of Reims and were expelled from the *urbs*. The legates of the church of Reims returned from Rome, bringing back with them from Pope Stephen the *pallium* for [Arch]bishop Hugh. They also went to the *principes* of the kingdom, so that they might receive Louis as king and send their own legates to Rome. But if this were not done by the Nativity of the Lord [25 December], they understood that they would then be excommunicated.

[24C] Lord Abbot Odo [of Cluny] worked with Hugh, the king of Italy, and Alberic, the Roman patrician, to make peace between the two. King Hugh tried to drive out the Saracens from their *munitio* of Freinet. Count Roger [of Laon], who was serving in a legation from King Louis to William [Longsword], the *princeps* of the Northmen, died there. William received King Louis in a royal manner at Rouen. Likewise, [Count] William of Poitou¹¹⁶ and the Bretons, with their *principes*,¹¹⁷ came to the king. With these men the king came to the river Oise, while Hugh [the Great] and Heribert [of Vermandois] encamped with Otho [of Verdun], duke of the Lotharingians.[118] After the bridges were destroyed and ships had been seized, along with the ships that they were able to take from the other side of the river, dissension was stirred up among them by the negotiators on each side and a truce was arranged to last from the middle of September until the middle of November. Hostages were exchanged, including Heribert's younger son, who was given to the king. The king [Louis] himself, along with William [Longsword] and Hugh [the Great], sent hostages to King Otto [of Germany] through Duke Otho.

[24D] There was a great famine through all Francia and Burgundy, along with an epidemic that struck cattle, and few animals of this type survived in these lands.

[24E] King Louis set out to meet King Otto and the two men received each other amicably and strengthened their friendship with a pact. Otto labored intensely to make peace between King Louis and Hugh [the Great], so that Hugh at last returned [his allegiance] to the king. Likewise, even Heribert [of Vermandois] and his son, also named Heribert, became [the men] of King Louis. When the king returned, the bishops of the province of Reims came to him, and Louis received [Bishop] Raoul [II] of Laon and restored his see to him.

[24F] The venerable Lord Abbot Odo [of Cluny], who had restored many monasteries and who had repaired the holy rule [of Saint Benedict], died at Tours and was buried at [the monastery of] St-Julien [of Tours].

25.

[25A] In the year 943, Count Arnulf [of Flanders] arranged for the treacherous murder of William [Longsword], the *princeps* of the Northmen, at a conference to which he had been called. King Louis then gave the land of the Northmen to William's son [Richard], born of a Breton concubine [Sprota]. Some of the *principes* of the Northmen committed themselves to the king, while others committed themselves to Duke Hugh [the Great].[119] Count Heribert [of Vermandois] died[120] and his sons buried him at St-Quentin. When they heard that Raoul, the son of Raoul of Gouy, had come into the lands of their father as if he were invading, they attacked and killed him. The news of this greatly saddened King Louis.[121] [Arch]bishop Artoldus left his monastery of St-Basle and set out for the king, who promised Artoldus that he would be returned to the diocese of Reims. Artoldus gathered up his brothers and other men who had been exiled from the bishopric of Reims, and they took possession of the *castrum* of Omont. King Louis and some others then attacked Mouzon, but Louis was driven off by *fideles* of Bishop Hugh [of Reims], and some of his men were killed. However, Louis burned some houses in the suburbs of this *castrum*, whereby much of the harvest was destroyed.

[25B] Hugh [the Great], the duke of the Franks, fought frequently against the Northmen who had come as pagans or had returned to paganism. They had killed a great many Christian footsoldiers (*pedites*) of Hugh's, but, with the agreement of the Christian Northmen who were holding the place, Hugh was able to take the *castrum* of Évreux, killing many of the Northmen and putting the others to flight. King Louis set out again for Rouen and killed the Northman Turmoldus, who had returned to idolatry and to heathen rites. Turmoldus had forced [Richard] the son of William [Longsword] and others to join him in this and he plotted against the king. Turmoldus joined with the pagan king Setricus and King Louis killed them [in battle]. King Louis then committed Rouen to Erluinus [of Montreuil] and returned to Compiègne. There Duke Hugh [the Great] waited for him, along with his nephews, the sons of Heribert [of Vermandois],[122] and this meeting was the cause of considerable tension.

[25C] With Duke Otho of the Lotharingians and Bishop Adalbero [of Metz] serving as mediators, with Duke Hugh [the Great] especially insistent, the king first received [Arch]bishop Hugh [of Reims], with the understanding that [St-Basle and Avenay] the abbeys that [Archbishop] Artoldus had renounced and turned over to the king would be restored to Artoldus, who would be provided with another bishopric. Moreover, the honors that the brothers and kinsmen of Artoldus had held from the diocese of Reims would be returned to them. After this was done, the other sons of Count Heribert were received by the king. Again King Louis set out for Rouen and he received Évreux from Duke Hugh [the Great]. However, the king fell ill at Paris and remained in bed for almost the entire summer.

[25D] [Arch]bishop Hugh captured the *castrum* of Ambly and burned it down. The brothers Robert and Raoul, who had been expelled from Reims, were holding Ambly and using it as a base for raids throughout the diocese of Reims. Erluinus [of Montreuil] engaged [Count] Arnulf [of Flanders] in battle and defeated him. He also killed the man who had killed William [Longsword], the *princeps* of the Northmen, and sent that man's amputated hands to Rouen. Likewise [Arch]bishop Hugh besieged the *munitio* of Omont, which was being held by Dodo, the brother of [Arch]bishop Artoldus. [Arch]bishop Hugh gave up the siege on the command of King Louis after taking Dodo's young son as a hostage.

[25E] Duke Hugh [the Great] took the daughter of the king from the baptismal font and the king delegated to him the *ducatus* of Francia.[123] The king [Louis] also subjected all Burgundy to his power (*dicio*). Likewise [Duke] Hugh [the Great] brought peace between the king and [Count] Arnulf, at whom Louis had been angry due to the murder of William [Longsword, *princeps* of the Northmen]. King Otto [of Germany] captured some of King Louis's *fideles* who had plotted against Otto, which led to ill will between the two kings.

26.

[26A] In the year 944, King Louis and Queen Gerberga set out for Aquitaine and spoke with Raymond, the *princeps* of the Goths[124] and, with other magnates (*proceres*) of Aquitaine, he [King Louis] returned into Francia. King Louis then gave to Ragenoldus[125] the *castrum* of Montigny-Lengrain, in the *pagus* of Soissons, which had belonged to the monastery of St-Crépin. A little before Louis had received the monastery from the sons of Heribert, who had returned it to him. The king's *fideles* captured Montigny-Lengrain from certain members of the garrison (*oppidani*) by an act of treachery. A man named Andrew, who was holding it in loyalty to the sons of Heribert, killed the traitor but was himself killed. Members of the king's household (*domestici regis*) took the *urbs* of Amiens, which Heribert's son Odo had been holding. Bishop Deroldus of Amiens had given his agreement to this and his own *fideles* had handed it over to him. Thus another conflict arose between the king and the sons of Heribert [of Vermandois].

[26B] Duke Otho of the Lotharingians departed from this life. Hugh [the Great], the duke of the Franks, made a peace pact with the Northmen after hostages were given and received by both sides. Then [Duke] Hugh set out with Heribert's sons to meet King Otto [of Germany] in Lothair's Kingdom. However, King Otto delayed his arrival and sent Duke Herman [of Swabia] with a large army.

[26C] After peace was made between Erluinus [of Montreuil] and Arnulf [count of Flanders], King Louis gave the *castrum* of Amiens to Erluinus. Heribert's sons took the *munitio* of Clastres, in the *pagus* of Vermandois, due to the treachery of Raoul, one of King Louis's *fideles*. This Raoul secretly slipped out of the stronghold when Heribert's sons entered it and plundered the treasures before abandoning the deserted *municipium*.

[26D] Duke Hugh sought to meet with Herman [duke of Swabia], who had been sent to lay siege to the *castella* of King Louis's *fideles*, Ragenarius and his brother Raoul. They did not have a fortified position (*praesidium*) from which they might resist Herman, and when many gifts had been given, they asked King Otto for his pardon. Otto went to the palace at Aachen and met with the Lotharingians, and the envoys of King Louis as well as the legates from Duke Hugh appeared there as well. Otto received Louis's legates but he was hostile to the duke's legates. However, Manasses, one of Hugh's envoys, saw that Louis's men were very opposed to his own legation's mission, in the middle of the meeting made public certain mandates recently given to him by Louis to be given to Otto, which previously he did not wish to reveal. He thus disclosed harsh rebukes that King Louis had ordered him to convey to King Otto because Otto had failed to live up the oaths that he had sworn to Louis, and Manasses added many additional insults to Louis as well. Otto's anger was thus aroused and, when Louis's envoys were unable to contradict what Manasses had said, he ejected them from his court and treated Hugh's representatives honorably and ordered his own *fideles* to desist from giving aid to Louis or from having contact with him.

[26E] In the Transrhenine regions of Germany there was a man who had one of his hands cut off, but, after fourteen years had passed, it was completely restored while he slept at night, just as those who knew him aver. In these same regions, fiery iron balls were seen in the air, which burned some houses and *villae* as they flew around. But in some other places they were repelled by setting up crosses, by holy water and by an episcopal benediction.

[26F] Royal soldiers plundered the diocese of Reims and Heribert's sons did the same to the lands of the abbey of St-Crépin [of Soissons], and Ragenoldus [of Roucy][126] sacked the lands of the abbey of St-Médard [of Soissons]. Thus they ran wild with either pillaging or plundering.

[26G] A powerful storm, with very strong winds, struck the *pagus* of Paris, demolishing the walls of a very old house, built with the strongest cement, which had stood intact for a very long time on Montmartre. It was said that demons in the form of horsemen were also seen there, which destroyed a nearby church when its beams were thrown against the walls of the house. The demons also uprooted the vines that grew on this hill and they destroyed all the crops.

[26H] Soon afterwards, the Bretons suffered a catastrophe. They were disunited due to a quarrel between the two *principes* [Judicaël] Berengar [count of Rennes] and Alan [Barbatorte, count of Nantes]. Even though the Northmen had made a pact [of peace] with them, they attacked the Bretons and massacred them. Their *civitas* of Dol was captured and its bishop was crushed and killed in the church by the great crowd of refugees. Finally the Bretons repaired their strength and fought against the Northmen, seeming to have overcome them. When a third battle was engaged a large number of men were killed on each side, but the Northmen won the victory, massacring the Bretons and pushing them out of their own land. These Northmen who invaded their lands had recently come over from across the sea.

[26I] King Louis marched into the land of the Northmen, along with Arnulf [count of Flanders], Erluinus [of Montreuil] and certain bishops of Francia and Burgundy. [Count] Arnulf advanced in front of the king and routed the Northmen who were keeping guard at Arques-la-Bataille, and he prepared the king's crossing of the river [Béthuen]. Thus King Louis reached Rouen and was received by the Northmen in the *urbs*, while those who were against receiving the king took to the sea, and all of the rest were subjugated to him. Duke Hugh [the Great], with his own supporters and with certain magnates (*proceres*) from Burgundy, journeyed across the Seine to Bayeux and beseiged that *civitas*. King Louis had given Bayeux to [Duke] Hugh if Hugh should aid the king in conquering this group (*gens*) of the Northmen. King Louis was received by the Northmen and he ordered Duke Hugh [the Great] to raise the siege of the aforesaid *civitas* [of Bayeux]. After Hugh departed, the king entered Bayeux. This led to the kindling of a quarrel between the king and the duke, as a result of which the king took hostages from Évreux that had been surrendered to Hugh and refused to return them to the duke.

27.

[27A] In the year 945, while King Louis still remained at Rouen, at Laon Queen Gerberga gave birth to a son,[127] who was named Charles for the purpose of instruction. The king returned to Laon and spoke with Arnulf [count of Flanders]. They resolved certain matters, and King Louis returned to Rouen. Count Bernard of Senlis, [Count] Theobald of Tours[128] and [Count] Heribert,[129] attacked the king's *castellum* of Montigny during Easter season.[130] They captured and burned it, making it indefensible. Likewise Bernard attacked the hunters and dogs of the king, and carried off their horses and whatever else belonged to them that he could find. He also attacked the *oppidum* of Compiègne, which was a customary royal residence, as well as some *villae* that were subject to the same place.

[27B] King Louis raised an army of the Northmen and they plundered the *pagus* of Vermandois. The king joined to his force Erluinus [of Montreuil] and some of the soldiers of [Count] Arnulf's, along with [Arch]bishop Artoldus and the men who had recently been expelled from Reims, as well as Count Bernard [of Réthel] and Count Theoderic, Bernard's nephew. This army laid siege to the *urbs* of Reims. The crops around Reims were plundered and part of them were burned, and many churches were wrecked. Frequent skirmishes were fought at the gates and around the wall of the city, and many were wounded, and some killed, on both sides.

[27C] Finally, Duke Hugh [the Great] engaged the Northmen who had invaded his territory and he routed them in a great slaughter, pushing them back beyond the borders of his lands. Hugh then sent a message to the king at Reims and gave hostages so that Ragenoldus [count of Roucy], representing the king, would come to a meeting with Hugh. When Ragenoldus departed, Hugh treated with him so that the king might accept hostages from [Arch]bishop Hugh and give up the siege of Reims, and so that [Arch]bishop Hugh might go to a *placitum* to provide the king with an explanation for whatever the king asked him. When all these concessions were thus given to him, the king raised the siege of Reims, which had lasted fifteen days. Therefore, around the feast of Saint John [24 June], Duke Hugh and the king participated in a *placitum* through intermediaries, but no sure peace was established. However, the two sides did agree to a peace until the middle of August. After all this, King Louis went to Rouen, taking Erluinus [of Montreuil] and some of his household troops (*domestici*) with him.

[27D] Lord Teotolo, the venerable [arch]bishop of the *urbs* of Tours, died. He had been working to make peace between the king and the *principes*. Occupied with this matter, he returned from Laon and was struck by a bodily illness on this journey. After he had breathed out his last breath, a sign of lights appeared coursing through the sky, which seemed to be about a cubit in length. This light was so bright that it dispersed the shadows of night and those who were carrying his body could perform the task. It was said that by this comfort they gained almost 200 miles and carried his body to the *urbs* of Tours. Teotolo was buried reverently in the monastery of St-Julien, which the same holy man had raised to the highest standards of [monastic] religion, next to the tomb of Lord [Abbot] Odo [of Cluny]. It was then declared that this temple was made famous by divine miracles.

[27E] While King Louis delayed at Rouen, the Northman Harold, who was in command at Bayeux, sent a mandate to the king, stating that he himself would come to meet with the king at a time and place that was agreeable. The king came to the place with only a few men, but Harold arrived armed, with a large number of Northmen. They attacked the king's companions and killed almost all of them. Only the king escaped through flight, followed by a certain Northman who was his faithful man (*fidelis*). The king came to Rouen and was captured by other Northmen whom he thought to be faithful to him and he was held under guard.

[27F] Hugh, the king of Italy, was deprived of his rule (*regnum*) by his own people and his son [Lothair] was received in the royal power (*regnum*). [Arch]bishop Hugh laid siege to the *castrum* of Omont and took it after a siege of almost seven weeks. Dodo [brother of Archbishop Artoldus] handed over the stronghold on the condition that this same archbishop acknowledge his son and the son of his own brother and concede to them the lands of their fathers. While Duke Hugh was involved with the matter of the capture of King Louis, the Northmen asked that the king's sons be given to them as hostages or they would not release the king. Therefore the queen was asked for the boys; she sent the younger one [Charles] but declared that she would not send the elder [Lothair]. Therefore, the younger boy was handed over to the Northmen so that the king might be set free, and, in addition, Bishop Guy of Soissons gave himself up as a hostage.

[27G] Therefore, the king was released by the Northmen and he was taken into custody by the *princeps* Hugh [the Great], who handed him over to Theobald [the Trickster, of Tours], one of his men. [Duke] Hugh then set out to meet King Otto [of Germany]. However, Otto did not want to speak with Hugh and instead sent Conrad,[131] duke of the Lotharingians, to him. [Duke]

Hugh spoke with Conrad and then returned, hostile to King Otto. When Bishop Richarius of Tongres died, King Otto gave his position to Hugh, the abbot of St-Maximin [of Trier]. However, Abbot Hugh was unwilling to be made bishop and ran away. Nevertheless King Otto had him ordained bishop and returned across the Rhine.

[27H] In the *pagus* of Paris and also in various *pagi* thereabouts, men were struck in various appendages with wounds of fire.[132] Gradually they were burned up and consumed until at last death finished the punishments. Some of those afflicted sought out many places of the saints and escaped the torments. Many were healed in Paris in the church of Mary, the Holy Mother of God [Notre-Dame of Paris]. All those who went there affirmed that they had been saved from that affliction. Duke Hugh [the Great] gave them food in daily stipends. Some wished to return to their homes, but there the fire began again and they returned to the church [of Notre-Dame] and were again freed of the torment.

Fig. 4. Seals of King Louis IV

From *Recueil des Actes de Louis IV, roi de France (936-954)*, ed. Maurice Prou and Philippe Lauer (Paris: C. Klincksieck, 1914) pl. 8.

28.

[28A] In the year 946, a conflict was stirred up among the sons of Count Heribert over the division of their inheritance. However, through the mediation of their uncle, the *princeps* Hugh [the Great], they were pacified and the inheritance was divided in an agreeable manner.

[28B] King Hugh of Italy was received by his own people in the royal power (*regnum*).

[28C] Edmund, king of the English,[133] sent legates to the *princeps* Hugh [the Great] for the restoration of King Louis. The same *princeps* [Hugh] therefore held public meetings with his nephews[134] and with other magnates (*primates*) of the kingdom.

[28D] Pope Marinus [II] died and he was succeeded by Agapitus. Peace was made between the patrician Alberic and Hugh, the king of Italy.

[28E] Hugh, the duke of the Franks, received Hugh the Black, son of Richard [the Justiciar], and along with other dignitaries of the kingdom he restored King Louis in royal power (*regnum*) after the king had been held in custody for almost a year by Count Theobald [of Tours]. After this, Hugh received the *castrum* of Laon, which Queen Gerberga had been holding, and committed it to the same Count Theobald. Duke Hugh restored the royal honor and name to King Louis and committed himself to the king with the other magnates (*primores*) of the kingdom.

[28F] Edmund, the overseas king [of the English], died.[135] [Edith], the wife of King Otto [of Germany], the sister of this Edmund, also died.

[28G] Queen Gerberga recently sent a legation to King Otto, her brother, demanding help from him. Otto gathered a very large army from all of his kingdoms and, along with Conrad [the Peaceful], the king of Cisalpine Gaul [Upper Burgundy], came into Francia. King Louis went out to meet them and was received by them in a friendly and honorable manner. Then they all went to Laon but, after considering the strength of the *castrum*, they went away from it and attacked the *urbs* of Reims. They surrounded Reims with a siege, enclosing it with a large army. However, [Arch]bishop Hugh saw that he could not break the siege or resist such an immense army and took counsel with with some *principes* who seemed to be his friends, namely Arnulf [count of Flanders], who had married his sister,[136] Udo [count of Wetterau], whose wife[137] was his aunt, and Herman, Udo's brother, asking them what he should do. They advised him to go out with his men and surrender the *urbs* because the kings had decided to expel him completely, and if the *urbs* should be taken by storm, they would not be able to intercede with the kings to prevent his eyes from being torn out. This advice was received and shared with others, and, on the third day of the siege, [Arch]bishop Hugh left the city with almost all of the soldiers who had been with him. Thus the kings [Louis and Otto] entered the *urbs* with the bishops and the *principes* and they had Lord [Arch]bishop Artoldus, who had been ejected a little earlier, reinstalled. Archbishop Robert of Trier and [Archbishop] Frederick of Mainz received him and, with each of them taking one of his hands, they restored to him the same episcopal throne. Then the kings left Queen Gerberga at Reims and, with their armies, attacked the lands of Hugh [the Great], besieging the *urbs* of Senlis. However, they saw that it was very secure and, not wishing to take it by storm with the slaughter of their own men, they withdrew. The kings then crossed the Seine and pillaged heavily everywhere except for the *civitates*. They then crossed the land of the Northmen, devastating many places before returning to their own lands.

[28H] Bishop Deroldus of Amiens departed this life.

29.

[29A] In the year 947, the *princeps* Hugh [the Great] set out for the lands of Arnulf [count of Flanders] with his army that he had mobilized and besieged some of Arnulf's *munitiones*. However, as he expected no success, he returned home. King Louis, along with some Lotharingians, besieged Mouzon, which [Arch]bishop Hugh, who had been evicted from Reims, was now holding. However, Louis did not succeed in fulfilling his vows to take the place. After a month, the Lotharingians pulled back and Louis himself returned to Reims.

[29B] Bishop Bovo [of Châlons] died, and the people of Châlons chose the cleric Gibuinus, a young noble, to succeed him.

[29C] King Louis celebrated Easter [11 April] at Aachen with King Otto, who honored Louis with royal gifts.

[29D] The *princeps* Hugh [the Great] was persuaded to make a very presumptuous attack on the *urbs* of Reims, along with [Arch]bishop Hugh, as though it could be captured quickly. But this wish was ruined when the *fideles* of the king and of Archbishop Artoldus put up a resistance. On the eighth day after the attack began and looking foolish, Hugh withdrew.

[29E] [Arch]bishop Hugh, with the support of his uncle Hugh [the Great], ordained Theobald, a cleric of the church of Soissons, as bishop of Amiens.

[29F] At the wishes of Count Arnulf [of Flanders], King Louis and [Arch]bishop Artoldus set out for Arras and there joined with Count Arnulf. They then set out to besiege Montreuil, a *castrum* of Roger, the son of Erluinus [count of Montreuil and Ponthieu]. However, this failed and a number of men were killed and, seeing that the siege was hopeless, they returned home.

[29G] A great storm assailed Reims for an entire night, with continual lightning and shaking of the earth, so that wells were replenished and many houses were blown down.

[29H] At the beginning of August, the kings Louis and Otto celebrated the convening of a *placitum* on the river Chiers. The *princeps* Hugh [the Great] established his fortified encampment (*castra*) around Mouzon and Douzy. At the court, the bishops heard the dispute between Artoldus and Hugh, the [arch]bishops of the church of Reims. However, because a synod had not been called, the quarrel could not be resolved. A synod was arranged for the middle of November. In the meantime, the see of Reims was conceded to Artoldus, and Hugh, the other bishop, was permitted to stay at Mouzon. King Otto mediated a truce or armistice of the war between King Louis and the *princeps* Hugh [the Great], to last until the meeting of the synod.

[29I] Heriveus, the nephew of Heriveus, the former archbishop [of Reims], had built a *munitio* on the river Marne [Châtillon-sur-Marne] and now plundered the nearby *villae* of the diocese of Reims. [Arch]bishop Artoldus excommunicated him for seizing these goods of the church. Count Ragenoldus [of Roucy] and Dodo, the brother of [Arch]bishop Artoldus, went out with some soldiers of the church [of Reims] and drove off the bandits. When Heriveus received this news, he went out from his own *munitio* with his heavily armed soldiers against our men. However, he was killed along with some of his own men. All of the other men fled, with many wounded on each side. The victors took the body of Heriveus to Reims. [Arch]bishop Hugh left Laon and took with him Theobald [the Trickster, count of Tours] and many other wrongdoers. They came to Cormicy and other nearby *villae* at the time of harvest and stole almost all the grapes collected from the *villae* in various *pagi*.

[29J] The aforesaid synod was held at Verdun. [Arch]bishop Robert [II] of Trier presided, with the bishops Artoldus of Reims, Odalricus of Aachen, Adalbero of Metz, Goslenus of Toul, Hildebaldus from across the Rhine [bishop of Münster], and Israel the Breton in attendance, along with Abbot Bruno [of Lorsch], the brother of King Otto [of Germany],[138] Abbot Agenoldus [of Gorze] and also Odilo [abbot of Stavelot] also present, along with certain other venerable abbots. [Arch]bishop Hugh was summoned to this synod by the bishops Adalbero and Goslenus, who had been sent to bring him to the meeting. However, he did not wish to come. The entire synod judged that the diocese of Reims should be held by Lord [Archbishop] Artoldus. It was announced that another synod was to be held on 13 January.

30.

[30A] In the year 948, the aforesaid synod was held in the church of Saint Peter, within sight of the *castrum* of Mouzon, by Lord Robert [archbishop of Trier] and the rest of the bishops of the province of Trier,[139] along with some of those of the province of Reims.[140] [Arch]bishop Hugh came to the church and spoke with [Archbishop] Robert, but he did not wish to attend the synod.

He sent a letter from Pope Agapitus [II] to the bishops by one of his clerics who had brought it back from Rome. The letter contained nothing of canonical authority, but ordered that the diocese of Reims be returned to Hugh. When the letter was read out, the bishops took counsel with the abbots and with the rest of the wise men who were present. They responded that it was not worthy or acceptable to receive the command of the apostolic legation that Archbishop Robert had received from the hands of [Arch]bishop Frederick of Mainz in the presence of the kings and bishops of both Gaul and Germany, and he had considered part of this command, because he had let pass without interruption the letter that [Archbishop Hugh], the ambusher of [Arch]bishop Artoldus, was showing. On the contrary, what had begun according to the rules ought to be handled according to the canons. Thus it was ordered that the nineteenth canon of the council of Carthage,[141] concerning the accused and the accuser, be read out. When this was done, it was judged that, according to the meaning of this canon, [Arch]bishop Artoldus should retain the communion and the diocese of Reims (*communio et parrochia*) and Hugh, who had been summoned to two synods but had refused to comply, should abstain from the communion and rule of the diocese of Reims until he should come to a general synod, which was called for 1 August, to purge himself. Next, the bishops had this decision written down in a charter in their presence and they appended their decision to it and dispatched it to this same Hugh. After a day, Hugh sent the charter back to [Arch]bishop Robert, saying that he would by no means obey the judgment.

[30B] Count Arnulf [of Flanders], with the approval of the *princeps* Hugh [the Great], captured the *castrum* of Montreuil.

[30C] Meanwhile, Lord [Archbishop] Artoldus sent a letter of complaint to the Roman see. In response, Lord Pope Agapitus II sent his vicar, Bishop Marinus, to King Otto in order to convoke a general synod. Copies of this letter of this pope were sent from the Roman *urbs* especially to certain bishops of Gaul and Germany summoning them to the synod.

[30D] On 7 June the synod was convened by the command of Pope Agapitus [II] in the royal palace of Ingelheim at the church of Blessed Remigius, to deal with the serious dispute between King Louis and the *princeps* Hugh [the Great], and between Archbishop Artoldus of Reims and [Archbishop] Hugh, who had been illicitly substituted for him in the same *urbs*. These conflicts greatly disturbed the entire kingdom of the Franks.

[30E] Those who came for the celebration of the synod when the aforesaid Marinus, the vicar of the apostolic see arrived, were the bishops of Germany and the Gauls, namely Archbishop Robert of Trier, Artoldus of Reims, Frederick of Mainz, Wicfredus of Cologne, Adaldachus of Hamburg, Hildebaldus of Münster, Goslenus of Toul, Adalbero of Metz, Berengar of Verdun, Fulbert of Cambrai, Raoul [II] of Laon, Richoo of Worms, Reimboldus of Speyer,

Poppo of Würzburg, Conrad of Constance, Odelricus of Augsburg, Thethardus of Hildesheim, Bernard of Halberstadt, Dudo of Paderborn, Farabertus of Tongres, Lioptacus of Ribe, Michael of Regensburg, Dodo of Osnabrück, Everis of Minden, Baldricus of Utrecht, Herold of Salzburg, Adalbert of Passau, Starchandus of Eichstätt, Horath of Schleswig, Wichardus of Basle, and Liesdac of Ribe.

[30F] When all these bishops took their seats in the church of Saint Remigius, prayers were said before the mass, according to the procedure for the celebration of a council, and sacred authority was read out. The glorious kings Otto and Louis entered and took their seats. After the speech of the apostolic legate Marinus, King Louis rose from his side and, with the approval of King Otto, he recited his dispute in the presence of Marinus and the rest of the bishops gathered there. He recounted how he had been summoned from the regions across the sea by legates of [Duke] Hugh and the rest of the *principes* of Francia to receive the kingdom that was his inheritance from his father. By the oaths of all and by the acclamations of the magnates (*proceres*) and the soldiery (*militia*) of the Franks he had been raised and consecrated to possess the height of royal government. Afterwards, he had been driven out by [Duke] Hugh and he had been attacked by tricks and had been held in custody for an entire year by Hugh. He had been able to obtain his freedom only by giving up the *castrum* of Laon, which Queen Gerberga had held, along with her *fideles* gathered from all her royal residences, when Hugh was seizing the fortification. With all these evils that he had suffered after he had received the kingdom, if anyone should reproach him for what he had done, he would purge himself or defend himself in individual combat, according to the judgment of the synod and the command of King Otto.

[30G] Then Archbishop Artoldus rose and, according to the order of the Roman pope that had been given to him, he laid out an account of the origin and development of the conflict between himself and [Archbishop] Hugh over who should succeed as bishop of the church of Reims. After the letter had been recited to the kings, translated into the German language,[142] Sigbaldus, one of Hugh's clerics, entered the synod with a letter that he had brought from Rome and which he had already made public at the previous synod at Mouzon.[143] Sigbaldus asserted that the same letter had been given to him at Rome by the man who had been present with the vicar Marinus. This Marinus produced the letter that Sigbaldus had brought back from Rome and ordered that it be read out in the open synod. In the reading, it was discovered that Bishop Guy of Soissons, and also Hildegarius of Beauvais, Raoul [II] of Laon and the rest of the bishops of the province of Reims had sent letters to the Apostolic See so that Hugh might be restored to the see of Reims and Artoldus expelled from it.

[30H] After the letter had been read, [Arch]bishop Artoldus and [Bishop] Raoul [II of Laon] rose up, as did Bishop Fulbert of Cambrai, and disputed the contents of the letter, stating that they had never seen or heard it before, nor had they consented to the signing of the letter. Sigbaldus was not able to refute them, though he did attack them loudly with wild charges. Lord Marinus ordered the matter brought before the general council so that he might receive counsel and proper judgment concerning this man making such charges against the bishops. But the bishops of the synod, after the accuser had been shown publicly to have made false charges when the specific accusations had been read out, unanimously judged that he ought to be deprived of the office that he enjoyed and, according to the meaning of the chapters, he ought to be sent into exile. Therefore, he was reduced to the diaconate as an office he could exercise and, as a condemned man, he withdrew from the synod. The synod decreed, praised and confirmed that according to the meaning of the canons and the decrees of the holy fathers, the diocese of Reims should be retained by and handed over to Bishop Artoldus, who had been present at every synod and had not fled from the judgment of the synod.

[30I] On the day after the decision [8 June], after the recitations of divine authority and the speech by the vicar Marinus, Lord Archbishop Robert of Trier suggested that, because according to the institutes of sacred law[144] the diocese of Reims had been restored and reinstituted to [Arch]bishop Artoldus, the judgment of the synod ought to be executed against the one who had invaded that see. Therefore, the vicar Marinus ordered that the synod issue a decree against this presumption. Accordingly, it was commanded that the catholic canons of holy law be read out. Then, according to the institutes of sacred canons and the decrees of the holy fathers Sixtus, Alexander, Innocent, Zosimus, Boniface, Celestine, Leo, Symmachus[145] and the rest of the holy doctors of the church of God, they excommunicated and removed from the bosom of the church of God the aforesaid Hugh, the invader of the church of Reims, until he should do penance and make worthy satisfaction.

[30J] The remaining days of the synod were spent on other important matters concerning incest in marriages and churches in Germany that had been sold improperly and illicitly taken away by lay people and given to priests. This was prohibited and it was decreed that no one at all should presume to do this. Concerning other matters of need for the church of God, many other things were decided.

[30K] Meanwhile, King Louis sought from King Otto assistance against [Duke] Hugh [the Great] and his other enemies. Otto granted Louis's request and ordered Duke Conrad [the Red, of Lotharingia] to advance with the army of the Lotharingians in aid of King Louis. Meanwhile, as the army was being gathered, King Louis remained with Duke Conrad [of Lotharingia], and the bishops Artoldus [of Reims] and Raoul [II of Laon], who were with the king, went to be with the Lotharingian bishops lest they should encounter opponents on the road. Therefore, we[146] stayed with [Archbishop] Robert of Trier, [Bishop] Raoul [II] of Laon, and with [Bishop] Adalbero of Metz for almost four weeks. When the army at last had been gathered, the Lotharingian bishops went to Mouzon and besieged and attacked that *castrum.* They forced the soldiers there with Hugh [the deposed archbishop of Reims][147] to surrender. After they took hostages from these men, they set out to meet King Louis and Duke Conrad in the *pagus* of Laon. Therefore, the duke [Conrad] and the army laid siege to the *munitio* of Montaigu that had been built by Theobald [the Trickster, count of Tours], who was also holding it. In addition, Theobald was holding Laon against the king. The army quickly captured the *oppidum* and then advanced to Laon. The bishops gathered in the church of Saint Vincent [in Laon] and excommunicated this Theobald. Also, on behalf of Marinus, the legate of the Apostolic See, by letter they summoned the *princeps* Hugh [the Great] to come to make amends for the evils that he had done against the king and the bishops. Finally, Bishop Guy of the *urbs* of Soissons came to King Louis and committed himself to the king and was reconciled with Archbishop Artoldus, making satisfaction to the archbishop for having ordained [Archbishop] Hugh.

[30L] Duke Conrad [of Lotharingia] raised the daughter of King Louis from the sacred font [of baptism].

[30M] When the *castrum* of Mouzon had been taken and demolished, the Lotharingians returned home.

[30N] Therefore Hugh [the Great] made no delay and gathered many of his own men and a contingent of Northmen at Soissons and besieged the *urbs.* He killed many of the defenders and burned the house of the mother church[148] by putting fires to it. He also burned the canons' cloister and part of the *civitas.*[149] However, he was not able to capture the *civitas* and he gave up the *urbs.* He came to a *munitio* that Ragenoldus [count of Roucy], one of King Louis's counts, had built at Roucy on the river Aisne, vallating[150] the unfinished munitio. However, [Duke] Hugh was unable to take it, but he plundered the *villae* of the church of Reims that were close by his camp (*castra*). Hugh's thieves killed many of the dependents (*coloni*), violated churches and raged so furiously that in the village (*vicus*) of Cormicy they killed almost forty men around the church and plundered that temple of everything. Then, after many offenses had been committed, Hugh and his thieves returned. Thus, the soldiers who had been with the excommunicated [bishop] Hugh up to this point returned to [Arch]bishop Artoldus. The bishop received many of them after they returned the goods that they had taken, but some of them he refused to receive.

[30O] After these things were done, [Arch]bishop Artoldus set out to a synod at Trier with bishops Guy of Soissons, Raoul [II] of Laon and Wicfredus of Thérouanne.[151] When they arrived, they met with Marinus and Archbishop Robert [of Trier], who were awaiting them. However, none of the Lotharingian or German bishops were there. These bishops now sat down together and the vicar Marinus questioned them concerning what the *princeps* Hugh [the Great] had done after the previous synod with regard to them or to King Louis. They gave an account of the things mentioned above, of the evils that he had inflicted on them and their churches. Marinus asked about the summoning of this *princeps* [Hugh the Great and] whether or not they had actually sent the letter of summons to Hugh that he had ordered. The answer was given by Archbishop Artoldus, who responded that some of it had been sent but that some of it could not be delivered to Hugh because his thieves had intercepted the bearer of the letter. Nevertheless he had been summoned both by letter and by intermediaries in person. They inquired if there were a legate present at the synod on Hugh's behalf. However, no such person was found and it was decided that they would wait for one in case he should appear on the next day. When this did not happen, all who were present, both clerics and renowned members of the laity, clamored for [Duke] Hugh's excommunication. The bishops decided to delay his excommunication until the third day of the synod. A decision was made concerning those bishops who had participated in the ordination of [Archbishop] Hugh, who had been summoned but had delayed their arrival at the synod. Guy of Soissons confessed his guilt and prostrated himself in the presence of the vicar Marinus and Archbishop Artoldus. Archbishop Robert [of Trier] and Archbishop Artoldus [of Reims] interceded with Marinus so that [Bishop] Guy might be absolved, and he was absolved from this wrong. Wicfredus of Thérouanne[152] was found not to have been guilty of that ordination. The legate of Bishop Transmarus of Noyon, a priest,[153] added that his bishop had fallen seriously ill and could not attend the synod, and our bishops who were present attested to this.

[30P] On the third day, especially due to the insistence of Liudulfus,[154] King Otto's legate and chaplain, and also because King Otto wished it to happen, Count Hugh [the Great],[155] the enemy of King Louis, was excommunicated because of the evils that he perpetrated, as already mentioned. This sentence should last until he should come to his senses and make satisfaction in the presence of the vicar Marinus and the bishops whom he had injured. But if he should reject this, he should go to Rome for his absolution. Also excommunicated were two false bishops, who had been ordained by [the deposed archbishop] Hugh, who had been condemned. They were Theobald [of Amiens] and Ivo [of Senlis]. Theobald had been established bishop in the *urbs* of Amiens after [Bishop] Hugh had been expelled, and Ivo had been established bishop at Senlis after [Archbishop] Hugh's condemnation. Also excommunicated was Adelomus, a cleric of Laon, who was accused by Raoul [II], his bishop, of having introduced the excommunicated Theobald into the church. Bishop Hildegarius of Beauvais was summoned by a letter of the vicar Marinus and instructed either to come to the vicar or to go to Rome to answer to the lord pope for his presence at the illicit ordinations of those pseudo-bishops. Heribert [the Elder], the son of Count Heribert [II of Vermandois], was summoned to the synod to give satisfaction for the evils that he had committed against the bishops.

[30Q] When these actions were taken, the bishops returned home. King Otto's chaplain Liudulfus escorted the vicar Marinus to his king in Saxony, where he was to consecrate the church of the monastery of Fulda.[156] Following the consecration, Marinus returned to Rome after the winter had passed. In this year the bishops Geruncus of Bourges and Raoul [II] of Laon died. A son was born to King Louis, whom Bishop Artoldus raised from the sacred font and gave the name of his father.[157]

31.

[31A] In the year 949, the people of Laon, who were constant in their loyalty to King Louis, chose as their bishop the deacon Rorico, King Louis's brother,[158] and Archbishop Artoldus consecrated him bishop at Reims. However, Rorico was not received at Laon and took up his residence at the *munitio* of Pierrepont.

[31B] The people of Amiens detested Theobald, whom [the deposed archbishop] Hugh had established as their bishop, and they handed over the *castrum* to Count Arnulf [of Flanders]. Arnulf asked King Louis for assistance and captured the *oppidum* and expelled Theobald. He then introduced Ragembaldus into the diocese [of Amiens], a monk from Arras, whom the people of Amiens had previously chosen as bishop. Ragembaldus was brought to the king at Reims and was ordained bishop by Archbishop Artoldus. The *munitio* of Omont, which was being held by Lord [Arch]bishop Artoldus's brother Dodo, was captured in an act of betrayal by soldiers of this church of Reims, who had not been received by this bishop. They then summoned the excommunicated [Archbishop] Hugh into the *oppidum* and received him there. They proceeded to raid savagely the *villae* of the diocese that lay nearby.

[31C] Because the solemn day of Easter [22 April] was imminent, Queen Gerberga set out to her brother, King Otto. She celebrated Easter with him at the palace at Aachen, where legations of different peoples, that is, of the Greeks, Italians, English and others, were present.

[31D] The queen returned to Reims with her brother's promise of assistance, and King Louis suddenly attacked Laon. During the night Louis's men secretly scaled a wall. When the bars of the gates had been broken, the king entered the *oppidum* and captured the guards (*custodes*), except for those who had climbed up the tower of the royal residence that he himself had built at the gate of the *castrum*. Louis was unable to take the stronghold and cut it off from the *civitas* by throwing up a wall from inside. When Count Hugh [the Great] learned of these events, he set off to Laon with his men, while King Louis sent a legation to ask Duke Conrad of the Lotharingians to help him. Hugh [the Great] drew near the tower and established his camp in front of the gate. After installing garrison troops in the citadel with sufficient supplies, he withdrew from the hill. Therefore King Louis met with [Duke] Conrad, who spoke with Louis and arranged a truce of war between the king and Hugh [the Great] to last until the month of August. Meanwhile, Louis set out to speak with King Otto [of Germany]. After this was done, Louis returned to Reims. There Adalbertus, the son of [the late Count] Heribert [of Vermandois], came to Louis and became his man. Count Ragenoldus [of Roucy] was joined by some of the *fideles* of [Arch]bishop Artoldus and constructed the *munitio* of Mareuil on the river Marne. The *castrum* of Coucy-le-Château was handed over to Lord [Arch]bishop Artoldus by the men who were guarding it for Count Hugh [the Great] and [Count] Theobald [the Trickster, of Tours], and they committed themselves to the archbishop [Artoldus]. Dodo, the brother of Lord [Archbishop] Artoldus, and the bishop's *fideles*, along with Count Theoderic [of Réthel] laid siege to the *praesidium* of Omont, which the former [arch]bishop Hugh and his men had entered and were now holding. The besiegers established and fortified their camp in front of the gate of this *castrum*.

[31E] Count Hugh [the Great] gathered many of his own men and a band of Northmen and came to Laon. There he relieved the men who were holding the house on the citadel and replaced them with other men, along with sufficient supplies. From Laon, he set out into the *pagus* of Porcien and established his camp above Chaudion. From there he sent a message to King Louis, who was at Reims, appearing to seek peace. But, meanwhile, he suddenly attacked Laon in an effort to take the city. However, this attempt failed and he returned home. King Louis summoned Arnulf [count of Flanders] and some Lotharingians and pursued Hugh [the Great] all the way into the *pagus* of Senlis. Arnulf burned the suburb of this *civitas* and then returned home. Therefore Hugh [the Great] gathered a large army consisting of both Northmen and his own men and entered the *pagus* of Soissons. He sent the bishops Guy of Auxerre and Ansegisus of Troyes to the king and summoned Count Ragenoldus [of Roucy] to come to him. After oaths were sworn on each side, a truce was agreed to that would last until the Octave of Easter [14 April 950]. Soon afterwards King Louis spoke with [Count] Arnulf. Count Ragenoldus [of Roucy] captured the *castrum* of Châtillon-sur-Marne, which had previously belonged to [Archbishop] Heriveus [of Reims], when its wall was climbed at night. Dodo, the brother of Lord [Archbishop] Artoldus, took Omont after three days' effort by a similar means.

[31F] Pope Agapitus [II] held a synod at Saint Peter's, in the course of which the condemnation of [the deposed] bishop Hugh at Ingelheim was confirmed and the *princeps* Hugh [the Great] was excommunicated until he should give satisfaction to King Louis.

[31G] A certain Bernard, who belonged to the faction of Hugh [the Great] and who held the *castellum* of Chauny on the river Oise, committed himself as well as this *castellum* to Count Adalbert [of Vermandois].[159]

[31H] The church of Saint Mary, located on the stream called the Arne, shone with clear miracles as health was bestowed. Likewise the church of Saint Mary on the stream called le Py[160] shone with almost the same splendor.

32.

[32A] In the year 950, King Louis set out across the Meuse to seek advice and assistance from King Otto [of Germany] so that peace might be made between himself and Hugh [the Great]. Otto promised to send Duke Conrad [the Red] with the Lotharingians to Louis in order to accomplish this. Duke Conrad came with bishops and counts and conferred with Hugh [the Great] about making peace. He informed King Louis that he found Hugh agreeable and returned to King Otto after sending certain of the counts to make the king's will known to Hugh. Thus King Louis and the *princeps* Hugh [the Great] brought their forces to the Marne to make peace. Each one was on a different side of the river and representatives were sent back and forth, with Duke Conrad, Hugh the Black [duke of Burgundy], and the bishops Adalbero [of Metz] and Fulbert [of Cambrai] serving as mediators. Hugh [the Great] came to the king and made himself the king's man and was reconciled with Count Arnulf [of Flanders], Ragenoldus [count of Roucy], and Archbishop Artoldus [of Reims]. Thereupon Hugh [the Great] returned the tower of Laon to the king.

[32B] After these things had been accomplished, Hugh [the Great] had another meeting with the king at Compiègne, whereupon the episcopate of Noyon was given to Raoul,[161] an archdeacon of the same church, whom the people of Noyon had chosen to be their bishop.

[32C] Not long afterwards Hugh the Great took his army to the *urbs* of Amiens and he was received into the tower that Bishop Ragembaldus [of Amiens] was holding. Hugh then besieged another tower, which was held by the men of Count Arnulf [of Flanders]. King Louis lay ill at Laon.

[32D] King Otto [of Germany] laid siege to Prague, the great *urbs* of the

Wends. He received their king in subjection and made the Magyars submit to him.[162]

[32E] The men of Count Ragenoldus [of Roucy] captured the *munitio* of Braisne on the river Vesle, belonging to the church of Rouen, by means of a secret entrance. This enraged the *princeps* Hugh [the Great] and he sent a message to King Louis. Louis set out for that place and expelled the invaders, returning the *castrum* to the previous garrison (*custodii*). He then sought a meeting with Hugh [the Great] and when it was concluded, the garrison (*custodes*) of the *castrum* of Coucy-le-Château, which had deserted [Arch]bishop Artoldus, received Count Theobald [the Trickster, of Tours] into it. This angered the king, who asked Hugh [the Great] to hand the *munitio* over to him. But Count Theobald put up a great resistance and Louis was not able to obtain it. The king, now hostile, returned to Laon without consulting Hugh. [Count] Theobald expelled from Coucy many of those whom he found there.

[32F] After Raoul's election as bishop of Noyon,[163] he was ordained by Lord [Archbishop] Artoldus [of Reims]. Berengar, a *princeps* of Italy,[164] was made king of Italy when, as they say, King Lothair died by poisoning.[165]

33.

[33A] In the year 951, King Louis set out for Aquitaine with an army. However, before he entered that province, Charles Constantine, the *princeps* of Vienne, and Bishop Stephen of Clermont came to him and made themselves his men. Bishop Stephen honored the king with lavish gifts and William [Towhead] of Poitou [also duke of Aquitaine] came to meet him. While the king put off entering Aquitaine, he fell seriously ill. Letoldus [of Mâcon], a Burgundian count who had newly become the king's man, received Louis and looked after him well in this illness. When the king regained his strength, he returned to Francia.

[33B] Meanwhile, Frederick, the brother of Bishop Adalbero [of Metz], who was betrothed to the daughter of the *princeps* Hugh [the Great],[166] entered this kingdom [of Francia] and, without consulting either the king or the queen, began constructing a *munitio* at Fains. He frequently plundered around that place, which led King Louis, who was greatly annoyed, to send his delegation to King Otto [of Germany]. Otto invited the *princeps* Hugh [the Great] to come to him, which he did, sending two lions in advance to Otto and he himself followed close behind. The king received Hugh honorably during the Easter season.[167] Hugh, being treated properly by [King] Otto, stayed there at Aachen as he and Otto celebrated Easter day [30 March]. He received many gifts from Otto and, with Duke Conrad [the Red, of Lotharingia] escorting him as far as the river Marne, he returned home.

[33C] Duke Conrad [the Red], hostile to some of the Lotharingians, demolished the towers of some Lotharingians and deprived certain men of Verdun of their honors. He captured one *castellum* of Count Ragenarius[168] and besieged others of his.

[33D] King Louis's legates returned from King Otto and reported that Otto did not want Frederick or any other of his men to hold any *castrum* in this kingdom [of Francia], and in fact he forbade it unless King Louis should give his consent.

[33E] The Magyars left Italy, crossed the Alps and invaded Aquitaine, staying there almost the entire summer. They exhausted that region with their plunderings and killings and then returned through Italy into their own land.

[33F] King Louis laid siege to the *munitio* of Brienne-la-Vielle, which had been fortified by the robbers Gotbertus and his brother Angilbertus. He took the stronghold, whose defenders had been weakened due to want and famine, and demolished it. He then returned and set out to meet Arnulf [count of Flanders] and Hugh [the Great]. Hugh was hostile to Arnulf because the latter had occupied the *castrum* of Montreuil and the former lands of Erluinus [of Montreuil][169] and did not wish to attend the meeting. Instead, he and Roger[170] invaded this land and laid siege to a *castrum*.[171] At [Count] Arnulf's suggestion, King Louis sent a message to Hugh [the Great] and had the siege ended. Louis arranged a truce between Arnulf and Hugh to last until the first of December.

[33G] Queen Ottobega,[172] the mother of King Louis, left Laon escorted by men of the brothers Heribert and Adalbert[173] to meet with Heribert. Heribert received her and then married her, which greatly angered King Louis. The king took the abbey of Saint Mary,[174] which she was holding in Laon, and gave it to his wife Gerberga. Moreover, he brought the fisc of Attigny under his domination.

[33H] King Otto [of Germany] moved into Italy. At his coming, Berengar, the king of the Lombards, fled Pavia, which Otto entered, and married [Adelaid], the wife of the deceased King Lothair. She was the sister of Conrad, the king of Jura [Upper Burgundy].

[33I] The Saracens blockaded a passage of the Alps and took tribute from travelers on their way to Rome, who then were allowed to pass.

34.

[34A] In the year 952, King Otto [of Germany] sent a legation for his reception at Rome. When this was unsuccessful, he returned home with his wife [Adelaid], leaving some of his men to guard Pavia.

[34B] [King] Louis and Queen Gerberga returned to Laon. King Berengar [of Italy] went to Duke Conrad [of Lotharingia], who had remained in Pavia. He was received into [King] Otto's faith by Conrad and was taken to King Otto. Otto received Berengar in a kindly manner, conceded to him certain things in Italy as he thought best and permitted him to return in peace. After Otto celebrated Easter [18 April] he returned to Pavia.

[34C] Count Hugh [the Great] and his men came to the river Marne, and Duke Conrad [of Lotharingia] and some Lotharingians hurried to meet him there. Together they laid siege to the *munitio* of Mareuil, recently built in the river by Count Ragenoldus [of Roucy] and men of Lord [Arch]bishop Artoldus. The attackers constructed many machines and pressed the siege vigorously. After suffering losses they were able to capture the place and they burned it. The defenders were allowed to depart in [Duke] Conrad's faith. In the meantime, the nephews of Hugh [the Great], Heribert and Robert,[175] constructed the *munitio* of Montfélix. Thus Hugh [the Great] and [Duke] Conrad returned to their homes.

[34D] Without delay King Louis and Archbishop Artoldus set out, along with Count Ragenoldus [of Roucy], for the *munitio* on the river Marne that Hugh and Conrad had burned [Mareuil]. They repaired it and placed a large garrison (*custodes plures*) there. Then the king and Ragenoldus [of Roucy] set out for the vicinity of the *castrum* of Vitry-en-Perthois. This fortification was being held by Walter,[176] who had recently defected from the king and submitted himself and the *castrum* to Heribert [the Elder].[177] Louis and Ragenoldus pillaged and burned his *villae* and attacked the fisc of Ponthion. The king built another *munitio* against Vitry and placed some of the *fideles* from among the companions of Walter there as a garrison. He committed this *munitio* to Odalricus, an abbot from Burgundy, and returned to Laon. He immediately returned to Reims with the queen.

[34E] Archbishop Artoldus expelled the clerics who were serving at the monastery of St-Basle and sent monks into it. He then committed it to the [joint] abbots Hincmar and Rotmar.[178]

35.

[35A] At the beginning of the year 953, the *princeps* Hugh the Great sent legates to King Louis to confirm the peace and concord between them and asking for a meeting with Queen Gerberga. This was done and she returned to Reims, honored by gifts from him. Hugh gained the king's concession that the *castrum* that had been built against Vitry would be demolished. Thus the king and Hugh entered a *placitum* of concord and peace at Soissons in the middle of Lent.[179]

[35B] Meanwhile, a conflict had arisen between King Otto [of Germany] on the one side and his son Liudolf [duke of Swabia], Duke Conrad [of Lotharingia], and some of the magnates (*primates*) of his kingdom on the other. It came about when a son[180] was born to Otto and his new wife [Adelaid] and Otto promised his kingdom to his new son and he had his magnates (*magnates*) swear an oath of faithfulness to him. This was the same kingdom that he had earlier delegated to Liudolf before his invasion of Italy.[181] Therefore, the king removed Conrad from the duchy of Lotharingia and Conrad tried to capture Otto. The king learned of this and moved carefully, seeking Conrad's destruction. However, Conrad began to fortify his *oppida*. Ragenarius [III of Hainault], his long-time enemy, besieged a very well fortified *castrum* of his. Therefore Conrad gathered as large a body of soldiers as he could and hurried to loosen the siege. When the two forces met, many were killed on each side. Conrad fled to the *urbs* of Mainz.

[35C] Meanwhile, Queen Gerberga gave birth to twins at Laon, named Charles[182] and Henry. However, Henry died soon after his baptism.

[35D] A synod of five bishops met at St-Thierry in the territory of Reims, with Archbishop Artoldus presiding. Count Ragenoldus [of Roucy] was summoned there because of the ecclesiastical goods that he had stolen, but he did not wish to appear. He asked the king to intervene with the synod to prevent his excommunication. At Louis's request, the excommunication was dropped.

[35E] King Otto laid siege to the *urbs* of Mainz, to which Conrad [of Lotharingia] had retreated. After almost two months, Conrad came out and spoke with the king. After receiving hostages [from Conrad], Otto went back across the Rhine. After the citadel (*praesidium*) of Mainz had been cleared of his soldiers, Conrad immediately went to the *urbs* of Metz and made a secret entry into it. At the summons of his brother Henry [duke of Bavaria], [King] Otto went to Bavaria because of Liudolf's plunderings and his capture of some *urbes*. Conrad inflicted considerable devastation on the *urbs* of Metz and it is said that he then abandoned the city at the urging of Abbot Agenoldus [of Gorze].

[35F] [Arch]bishop Wicfredus of Cologne died and Bruno, King Otto's brother, was ordained bishop there. King Otto also committed to him the Lotharingian kingdom.

36.

[36A] In the year 954, the aforementioned [Duke] Conrad made an agreement with the Magyars and led them through the Lotharingian kingdom and into the lands of his adversary Ragenarius [III of Hainault] and of [Arch]bishop Bruno [of Cologne]. They plundered the area severely and, with considerable booty and many captives, they entered Louis's kingdom [of Francia]. They then passed through the *pagi* of Vermandois, Laon, Reims, and Châlons, and entered Burgundy. Many of them died, due both to battles and to sickness. The rest of them returned to their own land through Italy.

[36B] Louis, the son of the king, died at Laon.[183] King Louis left Laon and, as he was dying, went to the *urbs* of Reims. Before reaching the river Aisne, a

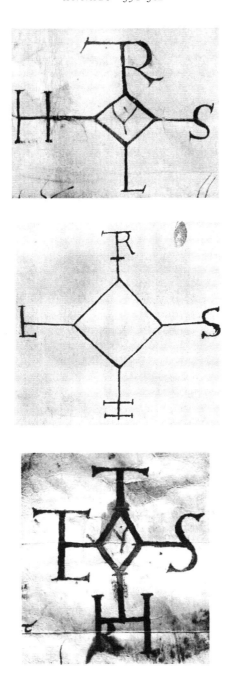

Fig. 5. Monograms of King Lothair ("Hlotharius")

From *Recueil des Actes de Lothaire et de Louis V, rois de France (954-987)* ed. Louis Halphen and Ferdinand Lot (Paris: C. Klincksieck, 1908) pl. 1.

wolf appeared ahead of him. He gave chase to it but when his horse was put to a gallop he fell off. Gravely injured, he was taken to Reims. He lay ill and weak for a long time and was aggrieved by elephantiasis. He was wasted by this disease and died. He was buried at [the monastery] of St-Rémi [at Reims].[184]

[36C] Queen Gerberga sent to Hugh [the Great], asking for his counsel and aid. Hugh met with her, receiving her honorably and consoling her. He made promises to her concerning the succession of her son [Lothair] to the king-dom.

[36D] Liudolf obtained the rule (*principatus*) of all Bavaria after his uncle Henry had been driven out. The Lotharingians were mauled by attacks of Duke Conrad and by the raids on each side.

[36E] Fulcharius, the dean of the monastery of St-Médard [of Soissons], was ordained bishop of Noyons at Reims. Frederick, the brother of Bishop Adalbero, married [Beatrice] the daughter of the *princeps* Hugh [the Great].[185] Count Heribert [the Elder][186] captured the *munitio* of Roucy by means of a sneak attack of some of his supporters (*satellites*).

[36F] The boy Lothair, son of Louis, was consecrated king at [the monastery of] St-Rémi by Archbishop Artoldus [of Reims], with the approval of the *princeps* Hugh [the Great], Archbishop Bruno [of Cologne], and the other bishops and magnates (*proceres*) of Francia, Burgundy and Aquitaine. Also, Burgundy and Aquitaine were given to Hugh [the Great] by Lothair. The *castrum* of Roucy was returned to Ragenoldus [of Roucy] and at the same time some *villae* were given to Heribert [the Elder][187] by Ragenoldus. Queen Gerberga returned to Laon with her son, the king.

[36G] Soon afterwards, soldiers of Ragenoldus [of Roucy] took [Count] Heribert's *munitio* of Montfélix, across the river Marne, in a surprise attack. Therefore [Count] Heribert [the Elder] and his brother Robert[188] laid siege to that and Heribert sent envoys to Ragenoldus at Reims so that he might have the *oppidum* returned to him. However, Ragenoldus refused until Heribert should break off the siege and they could come together to consider the *castra* that had been seized by both sides. When they met, Ragenoldus received the *villae* from [Count] Heribert that he had given to Heribert for the *castrum* and he returned the *oppidum* of Montfélix to Heribert.

[36H] Alberic, the patrician of the Romans, died and his son Octavian, a cleric, took up the rule (*principatus*) [of Rome].[189] After this, Agapitus died and Octavian was made pope of the *Urbs* [Rome] with the support of the Romans.[190]

37.

[37A] In the year 955, King Otto [of Germany] set out from his own lands and went out to meet the Magyars, who were plundering while they advanced. He fought and defeated them, preventing them from entering his realms (*regna*).

[37B] At Easter [15 April] the *princeps* Hugh [the Great] honorably received Queen Gerberga and her son, King Lothair, at Paris, and for many days he treated them honorably. He then set out into Aquitaine with King Lothair and advanced on the *urbs* of Poitiers. They did not find William [Towhead, duke of Aquitaine] there, and besieged the *urbs*. They kept up the siege for a long time but accomplished nothing. Count Ragenoldus [of Roucy] captured the *castrum* of Ste-Radegunde, situated next to the *urbs*, by a secret attack and burned it. However, after two months had passed and with the army suffering from lack of supplies, Hugh [the Great] broke off the siege. William [Towhead] had gathered his army and pursued the king's army. When [King] Lothair and Hugh [the Great] learned of this, they turned against him. William saw the size of his opponents' forces and fled. The royal battle forces (*regiae acies*) pursued him, killing many of his Aquitainians and capturing many of the nobles. William barely escaped with a few of his men.

[37C] A very large force of Magyars attacked Bavaria, seeking to invade Francia. King Otto [of Germany], along with Boleslav, the *princeps* of the Sarmatians,[191] and Conrad [of Lotharingia], who was now reconciled to the king, fought against them. He cut down the Magyars, almost annihilating them.[192] However, Conrad, who had fought very bravely that day and had inspired the king to victory, was killed.

[37D] After this war, King Otto fought against two kings of the Sarmatians[193] and with the support of King Boleslav,[194] who had submitted to him shortly before, he gained the victory.

[37E] Bishop Fulcharius [of Noyon] died and five months later Hadulfus, a cleric of Laon, was elected by the people of Noyon. He was ordained bishop at Reims by [Archbishop] Artoldus, Rorico [bishop of Laon] and Bishop Gibuinus [of Châlons].

38.

[38A] In the year 956, King Otto held a *placitum* with the Lotharingians at Ingelheim. He received hostages from them for almost all their *oppida*. Another *placitum* was held at Cologne after Easter [6 April]. There Otto received many treasures from the Lotharingians.

[38B] Soon a plague spread out over Germany and all of Gaul, with many dying and falling seriously ill with weakness. [Arch]bishop Robert of Trier,

Baldricus [bishop of Liège], and two other bishops immediately died of this plague.

[38C] King Lothair took by fighting a *munitio* on the river Chiers, which Count Ragenarius [of Hainaut] had seized from Ursio, a soldier of the church of Reims. Lothair captured the children of Ragenarius and some soldiers whom he found there, and then he burned and demolished the *castrum*.

[38D] The *princeps* Hugh [the Great] died.[195] Queen Gerberga met with her brother Bruno [archbishop of Cologne], at which meeting the soldiers and children of Ragenarius were returned. In addition, the dowry given to the queen by Duke Gislebert [of Lotharingia] were restored.

[38E] The episcopate of Trier was given to Henry, King Otto's kinsman. Bishop Fulbert of Cambrai died, and that see was given to Berengar, a cleric from across the Rhine and the nephew (*nepos*) of Bovo, the late bishop of Châlons.[196] Berengar was ordained at Reims by Archbishop Artoldus.

39.

[39A] In the year 957, one night in January, a little after the middle of the night, the church of the Holy Mother of God at Reims[197] was suddenly illuminated with a great brightness. Lord Archbishop Artoldus was present, and the custodian Withardus was amazed.

[39B] King Lothair set out for Upper Burgundy. A clamor for war had been raised between Bruno, the bishop who had become a duke,[198] and Count Ragenarius [Long-Neck][199] and other Lotharingians. Similarly, in Francia there was a cry for war between Baldwin [III], the son of Count Arnulf [of Flanders] and Roger [of Ponthieu], son of the late Erluinus, over the *castrum* of Amiens. Robert, son of Heribert [II of Vermandois] committed himself to King Lothair. King Lothair, along with his mother and his aunt [Hadwig], widow of Hugh [the Great], set out to meet his uncle Bruno[200] in the *pagus* of Cambrai. Ragenarius saw that he could not resist the great number that was coming against him and went to Bruno. However, Ragenarius did not want to provide the hostages that were asked for, so Bruno captured him and took him with him in custody. Soon afterwards, he exiled Ragenarius across the Rhine.

[39C] Liudolf, [King] Otto's son, who had gained almost all of Italy, died and was buried at the church of Saint Albinus in Mainz.

40.

[40A] In the year 958, some of the *fideles* of [Arch]bishop Artoldus captured the *castrum* of Coucy-le-Château in a surprise attack. Theobald [the Trickster, count of Tours] had committed that stronghold to Harduinus, one of his dependants (*subiectus*). When Harduinus saw that it had been captured, he fled into the citadel with his people, for that tower was very strong. King Lothair and Lord [Archbishop] Artoldus and many other bishops and counts came to Coucy in an effort to capture it, and they besieged the stronghold for almost two weeks. However, he accepted the nephews of Harduinus as hostages and raised the siege. Theobald [the Trickster] came to the *oppidum* but was not received there, and he returned home through the *pagi* of Laon and Soissons, plundering as he went. Theobald's men took the *munitio* of la Fère when some traitors handed it over to them. Bishop Rorico of Laon, along with soldiers of the church of Reims and others of his friends that he was able to gather up, laid siege to it. When King Lothair arrived and, through the mediation of the brothers Heribert and Robert,[201] he was able to get Theobald to order the return of the *castrum*.

[40B] King Otto made war against the Sarmatians.[202] Archbishop Bruno of Cologne set out through Francia into Burgundy with an army of Lotharingians in order to speak with his sisters [Gerberga and Hadwig] and his nephews.[203]

41.

[41A] In the year 959, [Archbishop] Bruno again came into Francia and at Compiègne met with his sister the queen and his nephews.[204] They were all quarreling over some *castra* that King Lothair had captured in Burgundy. After Bruno received hostages, he arranged a peace between them until a future *placitum* could be held.

[41B] King Lothair and the queen mother set out for Cologne during Easter season[205] and stayed there with his uncle [Archbishop] Bruno for that holy day. Lothair made assurances regarding the security of the kingdom of Lotharingia to his uncle, and Bruno gave gifts to him. Lothair then returned to Laon. The Lotharingians defected from Duke Bruno at the recommendation of Immo, who not long before had been Bruno's counselor but had recently withdrawn from him because Bruno had ordered some new *oppida* of the Lotharingians to be demolished. Moreover, it was said that he had imposed other new burdens on them. Bruno summoned these men to him and appointed Count Frederick [of Bar and Metz] over them in his place.

[41C] Count Arnulf [of Flanders] came to Reims and bestowed a large amount of silver on the church of Saint Mary,[206] which allowed the chests in which were contained relics of Saints Calixtus, Nicasius, and Eutropia and the rest of the saints, to be decorated and covered. In addition, he decorated a book of the gospels that belonged to this church with gold and silver, and he gave gifts to the monastery of St-Rémi [at Reims].

[41D] Count Robert[207] attacked the *castrum* of Dijon and the king's *fideles* were expelled. As a result, the king [Lothair] and queen [Gerberga] summoned [Archbishop] Bruno, who came into Burgundy with the Lotharingians and other peoples who had submitted to him. He laid siege to that stronghold, as well as to the *civitas* of Troyes, which Robert had also taken.

42.

[42A] In the year 960, Manasses, the nephew of Lord [Arch]bishop Artoldus, captured some traitors at the *castrum* of Omont, and they were sentenced to be hanged. There was even a priest among them. The *munitio* of Mézières, located on the Meuse within the land of the church of Reims, was returned to Archbishop Artoldus by Lantbertus,[208] who had been forbidden to hold it, in the presence of Frederick, the duke of the Lotharingians.

[42B] Richard, the son of William [Longsword], the *princeps* of the Northmen, married [Emma] the daughter of Hugh [the Great], the late *princeps* from

Fig. 6. Seal of King Lothair

From *Recueil des Actes de Lothaire et de Louis V, rois de France (954-987)* ed. Louis Halphen and Ferdinand Lot (Paris: C. Klincksieck, 1908) pl. 1.

across the Seine. [Count] Robert,[209] the brother of Heribert [the Elder], attacked and entered the *munitio* of Dijon, which the king's *fideles* were holding. He did this by pretending to be the king's *fidelis* and he then expelled the royal garrison (*regii custodes*). The king [Lothair] and [Gerberga] his mother, the queen, set out to recapture the *castrum* and laid siege to it. [Arch]bishop Bruno, along with the Lotharingians and the others who had submitted to him, arrived there. He took hostages from [Count] Robert and then handed them over to the king. One of the hostages, the son of Count Odelricus, was identified as a traitor, was judged, and was beheaded. The other hostage remained alive and was held. Odo and Hugh [Capet], the sons of Hugh [the Great], at the mediation of their uncle [Archbishop] Bruno, came to the king [Lothair] and were made his men. The king then established Hugh as duke and, in addition, gave him the *pagus* of Poitou that his father had held, with Burgundy being conceded to Odo.

[42C] However, [Archbishop] Bruno learned that some Lotharingians had risen up against him and he hurriedly returned there. The king and his cousins (*consobrini*)[210] took up the siege. Robert, one of Bruno's enemies, strengthened the *castrum* of Namur, while another one, Immo,[211] did the same to the *munitio* of Chièvremont. Bruno hurried to besiege it and found the area around it stripped of supplies, so he had to lay siege to an enemy that was well provisioned. Therefore a truce was arranged and he returned to Cologne. When Dijon had been taken, King Lothair placed his garrison in it and returned to Laon.

43.

[43A] In the year 961, Bishop Guy of Auxerre died.

[43B] Odo, the son of the late *princeps* Hugh [the Great], along with many magnates (*proceres*) of Francia and Burgundy, came to King Lothair in Laon during the Easter season.[212] At Soissons, a royal *placitum* and a meeting of various *principes* was held. In an effort to obstruct this, Richard, the son of the Northman William [Longsword], approached until he was met by some of the king's *fideles*. After a number of his own men were killed, Richard fled. The young man Hugh, the son of the late Count Roger [of Laon], died and was buried at [the monastery of] St-Rémi [at Reims]. Archbishop Artoldus of Reims died on 30 September. King Lothair, along with his mother Queen Gerberga and some of the magnates (*proceres*) of Francia, went to Burgundy, where some bishops and magnates (*primates*) from Aquitaine met him.

44.

[44A] In the year 962, Queen Gerberga obtained a meeting with her brother [Archbishop] Bruno, who suggested that the diocese of Reims not be given to Hugh [the deposed archbishop of Reims] as his brothers[213] were wanting.

[44B] King Otto [of Germany] went in peace to Rome. He was received there in an amicable manner and was elevated to the imperial honor there.[214] Then Berengar, the king of Italy, behaved unworthily and began to plunder and burn the regions which he should have governed.

[44C] King Lothair spoke with his cousin Hugh [Capet], who asked the king to restore the bishopric of Reims to the previously mentioned [former archbishop] Hugh. Then a truce was arranged to last until the middle of April.

[44D] A synod of thirteen bishops from the province of Reims and Sens met in the *pagus* of Meaux,[215] on the river Marne, under the presidency of [Archembaldus,] the bishop of Sens. Some bishops there attempted to restore the diocese of Reims to the often mentioned Hugh. However, this was opposed especially by Bishop Rorico of Laon and Bishop Gibuinus of Châlons, who argued that one who had been excommunicated by a great number of bishops could not be absolved by fewer number. Thus the matter was left to the judgment of the Roman pope.[216]

[44E] On the day of the Nativity of Our Lady, the Mother of God [8 September], a demoniac, a *servus*[217] of Queen Gerberga's, ran naked up the middle of the church to the altar, where he fell prostrate as being dead. At length, however, he rose up cleansed of the bad spirit. On that day as well a blind man named Harbertus received his sight there.

[44F] King Lothair spoke with the *princeps* Arnulf [count of Flanders] and arranged a peace between him and his nephew (*nepos*) also named Arnulf.[218] The count regarded the latter as hostile because he had killed his nephew's father, his own brother, after he had captured and killed him for his unfaithfulness. This *princeps* [Arnulf of Flanders] handed over to the king all his own land so that he might from this time forward be honored while he was alive.[219]

[44G] A certain man named Theobald fought against the Northmen but was defeated and escaped by flight. Therefore he considered his lord (*senior*) Hugh [Capet] to be hostile, so he went to the king [Lothair]. He was received by Lothair and Queen Gerberga and consoled with gentleness, and then he departed.

[44H] Abbot Vulfaldus of the monastery of St-Benôit-sur-Loire [Fleury] was made bishop of the *urbs* of Chartres. A legation from Pope John [XII] declared that the former [arch]bishop [of Reims] Hugh had been excommunicated by this pope, the entire Roman synod, and a synod held at Pavia. The legation's information was conveyed by Archbishop Bruno [of Cologne], and we[220] elected the illustrious cleric Odelricus,[221] the son of Count Hugh, to be

[arch]bishop of Reims, with the agreement of King Lothair, Queen Gerberga and [Archbishop] Bruno. Odelricus was ordained at Reims by the bishops Guy of Soissons, Rorico of Laon, Gibuinus of Châlons, Hadulfus of Noyon, and Wicfredus of Verdun.

45.

In the year 963, Archbishop Odelricus of Reims summoned the magnates (*proceres*) of Francia who had occupied certain possessions of the church of Reims. Therefore, although broken by age and weakened with infirmity, I resigned the ministry of my ecclesiastical dignity in the presence of this bishop. He freed me, in the seventieth year of my life, of this yoke and, in an election by our brothers, imposed it on my nephew Flodoard. After Bishop Gibuinus had left the *urbs* of Châlons, the brothers Heribert and Robert[222] besieged it. At the conclusion of the market, they burned it. Soldiers had climbed a tower there, and they were freed.

46.

[46A] In the year 964, the winter was very long and harsh until the first of February.

[46B] Lord [Arch]bishop Odelricus excommunicated the magnate (*procer*) Theobald, because he had improperly obtained the *castrum* of Coucy-le-Château, which he was now obstinately holding, along with certain estates belonging to [the monastery of] St-Rémi [at Reims].

[46C] Count Heribert [the Elder][223] returned to the bishop the *villa* of Épernay and gained his friendship. When [Archbishop] Odelricus asked for the rest of the *villae* of the church of Reims that Heribert had seized, he complied without hesitation.

47.

[47A] In the year 965, Odo, the son of Hugh [the Great], who was in charge of Burgundy, died. Those who directed that land [of Burgundy] turned themselves to his brothers Hugh [Capet] and Otto the cleric.[224]

[47B] When the *princeps* Arnulf [of Flanders] died [27 March], King Lothair entered his land and, with the mediation of Bishop Rorico of Laon, the magnates (*proceres*) of this province submitted to the king. Lothair returned to Laon, his mother, Queen Gerberga, remained there with her son, the boy Charles.[225]

[47C] After Archbishop Odelricus [of Reims] received Épernay from Heribert [the Elder] and Coucy-le-Château from Theobald [the Trickster, count of Tours], he freed them from the bonds of excommunication. He then conceded the *castrum* [of Coucy-le-Château] to that man's [Theobald's] son, who had committed himself to the bishop.

[47D] Emperor Otto [king of Germany] returned from the *urbs* of Rome and came to Cologne, where he welcomed his sister Queen Gerberga, who had come to him with her sons, King Lothair and the boy Charles. Otto held a great *placitum* with them and many other magnates (*proceres*).

[47E] Pope Octavian [John XII], who had received Otto and blessed him with the governmental rule of the empire,[226] left the *Urbs* [of Rome]. The emperor [Otto I] frequently recalled him because he had been charged with irreligiousness, but the pope did not wish to be returned to Rome.[227] When a synod met at Rome, the emperor had John, an illustrious cleric of the same church [of Rome], elected by the Romans and ordained pope.[228] But when Otto returned to Pavia, Octavian was received back by the Romans, but he died soon thereafter.[229] While John was staying at Pavia with the emperor, the Romans elected Benedict, the notary of this church, who had consented to the election of John [XIII] and who had been one of his followers, and they had him ordained pontiff. Emperor Otto returned to Rome and summoned a large synod. John[230] was restored to his see and Benedict was deposed by the judgment of the entire synod of bishops. Otto led Benedict away with him and sent him into Saxony.[231]

48.

[48A] In the year 966, King Lothair married Emma, the daughter of the former Italian king.[232]

[48B] Archbishop Odelricus excommunicated Count Ragenoldus [of Roucy] because he was obstinately holding *villae* of the church of Reims. This same count and his men raided some places of this diocese and plundered and burned them.

NOTES TO THE TRANSLATION

1   The Horn of Gaul, that is, western Brittany, especially the Brest-Quimper peninsula.

2   In his *Hist. Remensis Eccl.* 4.14 (ed. Stratmann, 407), Flodoard states that of the magnates (*primates*) of the kingdom, only Archbishop Heriveus of Reims responded to King Charles the Simple's call for aid against the invaders, raising a force reported to consist of 1,500 armed men.

3   Henry I the Fowler, king of Germany 919-36.

4   Gislebert was the son of Ragenarius I, count of Hainault, a grandson of Emperor Lothair, and one of the leading magnates of Lotharingia (died 915).

5   That is, Laon, which rests on a crescent-shaped bluff standing 100 meters above the surrounding plain. It is still called the "Crowned Mountain" of France.

6   Later King Robert I, see below, 4E.

7   The treaty of Bonn, 7 November 922, *Les Annales de Flodoard*, ed. Philippe Lauer (Paris: Alphonse Picard et Fils, 1905) 6, n. 7.

8   Lotharingian magnates who had defected from Charles, see 2A, 2C; on Otho, see 7B and n.

9   6 March-21 April.

10 See above, 2C.

11 Goslinus had been a notary for King Charles since 13 August 913 and was consecrated bishop on 17 March 922 (Lauer, *Annales*, 7, n. 3).

12 Rudolf (or Raoul) II, king of Transjurane Burgundy (Upper Burgundy) 912-37 and king of Arles (Provence) after 933 (Lauer, *Annales*, 7, n. 6).

13 Berengar asked that the Magyars attack his enemies in Italy. See Liudprand of Cremona, *Antapodosis*, 2.61, in *Liudprand of Cremona, The Embassy to Constantinople and Other Writings*, ed. John Julius Norwich, trans. F.A. Wright (London: J.M. Dent; Rutland, VT: Charles E. Tuttle, 1993) 60.

14 Rothildis was the daughter of Charles the Bald and thus the sister of Charles the Simple's father Louis II. She married Count Roger of Maine, whose daughter was the first wife of Hugh the Great (Janet Nelson, *Charles the Bald* [London and New York: Longman, 1992] 311; Philippe Lauer, *Louis IV d'Outre-Mer* [Paris: Émile Bouillon, 1900; repr. Geneva: Slatkine Reprints; Paris: Honoré Champion, 1977] 304).

15 Raoul was married to Count Robert's daughter Emma.

16 These would seem to be different examples of atmospheric phenomena, including those of sun dogs (parhelia, also called false suns or mock suns), when the sunlight is refracted through ice crystals in the atmosphere, which can result in bright spots or arcs of light appearing on both sides of the sun, equidistant from it.

17 The *pagus Ribuarium* was immediately west and southwest of Cologne; the Rur [Roer] river runs between Aachen and Cologne.

18 Boso, the son of Richard the Justiciar and thus the brother of Raoul of Burgundy; Ricuinus was the count of Verdun.

19 See above, 4C.

20 13 July 923, at the monastery of St-Médard in Soissons (Lauer, *Annales*, 14, n. 3).

21 The count of Senlis, presumably the son of Bernard, brother of Heribert I of Vermandois (see pedigree no. 1); Lauer, *Louis IV d'Outre-Mer*, 5, Michel Bur, *La formation du comté de Champagne* (Nancy: Université de Nancy II, 1977) 89.

22 Daughter of King Robert I, see above, 4C n.

23 The son of Ricuinus, murdered by Boso, King Raoul's brother, see above, n. 18 (Lauer, *Annales*, 18, n. 5).

24 Rudolf II, king of Transjurane (Upper) Burgundy; the names Rudolf and Raoul are both derived from the Latin form Rodulfus. Flodoard here styles Rudolf as *alter Rodulfus*, distinguishing him from King Raoul of the Franks.

25 That is, the *danegeld*, tribute paid to the Northmen; *danegeld* had also been collected in 862, 866, 877, 884, 889, and 897. Rosamond McKitterick, *The Frankish Kingdoms Under the Carolingians, 751-987* (London and New York: Longman, 1983) 233.

26 Hugh of Arles, marquis and duke of Provence, future king of Italy. He was the son of Theobald, count of Arles and of the Viennois as well as *marchio* of Provence (Lauer, *Annales*, 23, n. 1), and son of Bertha, illegitimate daughter of King Lothair II of Lotharingia, see 8D.

27 Thus Flodoard accompanied Archbishop Seulfus and was an eyewitness to this meeting (Lauer, *Annales*, 20, n. 1).

28 Viscount of Auxerre, brother of Manasses I, count of Dijon.

29 Walo succeeded his father Manasses I as count of Dijon (920-24); he in his turn was succeeded by his brother Gislebert (924-52), who also became duke of Burgundy. At his death, Gislebert was succeeded by his brother-in-law Hugh the Black (Lauer, *Annales*, 21, n. 3), King Raoul's brother.

30 Count of the *pagus Lommensis*, which comprised the deaneries of Florennes and Thuin, the archdeaconry of Hainaut, the deanery of Chimay, and the archdeaconry of Famenne; it has been suggested that Berengar was the son of Adalard and grandson of Evrard, *marchio* of Friuli (Lauer, *Annales*, 21, n. 6).

31 On this raid, see Liudprand, *Antapodosis*, 3.1-4 (*Embassy to Constantinople*, 71-73).

32 See above, 6A.

33 The word *Sarmatae*, Flodoard's classicizing term, derived from Ptolemy and Pliny the Elder, for those dwelling to the east of the Germans, that is, the Slavs.

34 Boso, son of Richard the Justiciar, and Otho, son of Count Ricuinus of Verdun (see above, 5C and n.).

35 Son and successor of King Robert as *marchio* of Neustria.

36 See David Bates, *Normandy Before 1066* (London and New York: Longman, 1982) 9.

37 Leader of the Northmen of the Loire (Lauer, *Annales*, 24, n. 9).

38 Isaac had burned down a *castellum* belonging to Bishop Stephen, Flodoard, *Hist. Remensis Eccl.*, 4.19 (ed. Stratmann, 411).

39 The cathedral of Notre-Dame.

40 Manasses II the Younger, son of Manasses I of Dijon, brother of Walo and Gislebert; see above, 6B and n.; Lauer, *Annales*, 26, n. 3.

41 6 December 924 (Lauer, *Annales*, 26, n. 6); Mons Calaus is perhaps Chalmont (Lauer, *Annales*, 274).

42 Lent ran from 2 March to 17 April in 925.

43 Son of Ricuinus, count of Verdun since 923 (Lauer, *Annales*, 29, n. 5); and see 4A.

44 Arnulf I the Great, count or *marchio* of Flanders.

45 That is, Count Heribert's young son Hugh was elected, see below, 7G.

46 The sons of Baldwin II the Bald, count of Flanders (879-918), were Arnulf I the Great, count of Flanders (918-65), and Adalolf, count of Boulogne and Thérouanne (Lauer, *Annales*, 32, n. 5; Lauer, *Louis d'Outre-Mer*, 12, n. 7; David Nicholas, *Medieval Flanders* [London and New York: Longman, 1992] 21).

47 King Raoul agreed to Hugh's election and conferred the civil administration of the diocese on Count Heribert, Flodoard, *Hist. Remensis Eccl.*, 4.20 (ed. Stratmann 412).

48 Hugh had been elected archbishop at the insistence of his father Count Heribert; see above, 7F.

49 Abbo successfully gained papal approval of both the election and Count Heribert's mastery of the diocese, and Abbo was himself named as the ecclesiastical administrator of the diocese; Flodoard, *Hist. Remensis Eccl.*, 4.20 (ed. Stratmann, 412). Flodoard also stated that at this point Count Heribert deprived him and others who had not participated in Hugh's election of their lands and offices held from the diocese of Reims (*beneficia possessionum ecclesiasticarum*), *Hist. Remensis Eccl.*, 4.20.

50 Easter was on 2 April. The date given by Flodoard for this total eclipse is accurate; see Bao-Lin Liu and Alan D. Fiala, *Canon of Lunar Eclipses, 1500 B.C.–A.D. 3000* (Richmond, VA: Willmann-Bell, 1992) 122, no. 5886.

51 Probably Acfridus, the brother of William II the Young, count of Avergne and duke of Aquitaine, 918-26 (Lauer, *Annales*, 35, n. 3).

52 This Bertha was the daughter of King Lothair II of Lotharingia, grandson of Louis the Pious; see above, 6A.

53 Rudolf II of Upper Burgundy married Bertha, the daughter of Burchard II, duke of Swabia. Burchard died in Italy in 926 in support of Rudolf II's effort to regain the kingdom of Italy. Liudprand of Cremona provides an account of Burchard's death in his *Antapodosis*, 3.14 (*The Embassy to Constantinople*, 76-77). In addition to Hugh of Arles, Bertha's other sons were Boso of Arles and Guy, marquis of Tuscany.

54 Bishop Hugh I of Verdun, 923-25.

55 Probably Eberardus, count of Franconia, son of Conrad the Old (Lauer, *Annales*, 36, no. 2).

56 Heiluidis, mother of Raoul de Gouy, had as a second husband Robert, count of Laon (Lauer, *Annales*, 36, n. 4).

57 Roger of Laon (husband of Heiluidis) died the previous year.

58 William II died during the summer of 927, between April and September, probably before 3 June (Lauer, *Annales*, 38, n. 2).

59 Flodoard adds in *Hist. Remensis Eccl.*, 4.21 (ed. Stratmann, 413), that Heribert's son Odo had been held as a hostage by the Northmen and was returned to him only after Heribert and several counts and bishops of Francia had committed themselves to King Charles.

60 Lent ran from 27 February to 13 April in 928.

61 *Marchio* of Tuscany, the half-brother of King Hugh (see above, 8D n. 5).

62 Odalricus, who had been driven out of his diocese by the Saracens, thus succeeded Bishop Abbo of Sens as the ecclesiastical administrator of the see of Reims (see above, 7G and n.); Flodoard, *Hist. Remensis Eccl.*, 4.22 (ed. Stratmann, 414).

63 In the diocese of Reims.

64 Boso, brother of King Raoul (see n. 23 above), held possessions in Lotharingia and was also count of Perthois (Lauer, *Annales,* 42, n. 4).

65 Rothildis (n. 14 above) died 22 March 922; she was abbess of Chelles, paternal aunt of Charles the Simple; Hugh the Great married her daughter (Lauer, *Annales*, 43, n. 7; Lauer, *Louis IV d'Outre-Mer*, 304); Rothildis had been married to Roger, count of Maine (Nelson, *Charles the Bald*, 311) and thus was the mother of Hugh I, count of Maine (McKitterick, *Frankish Kingdoms*, 185, 309).

66 Marozia (Marocia), a diminutive of Mary, was daughter of Theophylact, who was called a senator of the Romans. She married Alberic, marquis of Spoleto, and had five children, including Alberic II of Spoleto and the future Pope John XI. After the death of Alberic, she married Guy of Tuscany. Following her removal of Pope John X from the papacy in 924, Marozia dominated Roman politics and succeeded in naming her son as pope. Her third husband was Hugh of Provence, which led to her being ousted from power by her son Alberic II in 932 (see below, 15A). On Marozia, see Eleanor Duckett, *Death and Life in the Tenth Century* (Ann Arbor: University of Michigan Press, 1971) 55–58.

67 7 October 929.

68 Probably the count of Montdidier (Lauer, *Annales*, 44, n. 9).

69 See Lauer, *Louis IV d'Outre-Mer*, 64, 69; Helmut Schwager, *Graf Heribert II. von Soissons, Omois, Meaux, Madrie sowie Vermandois (900/06–943) und die Francia (Nord-Frankreich) in der 1. Hälfte des 10. Jahrhunderts,* Münchener Historische Studien, Abteilung Mittlalterliche Geschichte, ed. Eduard Hlawitschka, vol. 6 (Munich: Verlag Michael Lassleben Kallmünz, 1994) 134.

70 In the corresponding text of the *Hist. Remensis Eccl.*, 4.23 (ed. Stratmann, 415),

Ansellus is called the *subditus*, subject or dependant, of Boso, rather than *vassalus*.

71 The cathedral of Notre-Dame.

72 The cathedral of Notre-Dame.

73 Count of Autun since ca. 924, the year of the death of his brother Walo; see above, 6B.

74 Count of Troyes and perhaps viscount of Sens (Lauer, *Annales*, 48, n. 6).

75 Arnulf I the Old (the Great), count of Flanders (918-965), son of Baldwin II (879-918) (Nicholas, *Medieval Flanders*, 39).

76 Here *civitas* must have the meaning of a fortified area; in the *Hist. Remensis Eccl.*, 4.24 (ed. Stratmann, 416), Flodoard specified that it was the soldiers of the church (*milites ecclesiae*) who gave themselves up to the besiegers.

77 Heribert's wife was Adele, the sister of Hugh the Great (Lauer, *Annales*, 51, n. 4; McKitterick, *Frankish Kingdoms*, 359).

78 Gislebert, son of Manasses, count of Autun, and Richard, count of Troyes, son of Garnier of Sens (Lauer, *Annales*, 52, n. 2).

79 Appointed bishop of Châlons by King Raoul; see above, 13H.

80 A fortification belonging to Heribert.

81 The dean of a monastery was an official subordinate to the abbot.

82 Thus Flodoard was unsure if the *pallium* had actually been dispatched by the pope himself or by Alberic, *Hist. Remensis Eccl.*, 4.24 (ed. Stratmann, 416).

83 The battle of Merseburg, 15 March 933.

84 Count of Réthel or of Porcien (Lauer, *Annales*, 55, n. 4).

85 Probably the Avranchin and Cotentin (Bates, *Normandy Before 1066*, 9).

86 The cathedral of Notre-Dame.

87 The largest triumphal arch of the Roman Empire, built in the second or third century, named for a nearby temple to Mars. It stands to the east of the cathedral of Reims.

88 That is, the Rule of Saint Benedict.

89 14 or 15 January 936 (Lauer, *Louis IV d'Outre-Mer*, 2).

90 A number of Bretons, including Alain Barbetorte, the son of Matuedoi, count of Poher, fled to England to escape the raids of the Northmen. They were received in England by King Athelstan, Alain's godfather. In 936 Alain and other exiles returned to Brittany, which they were able to regain from the Northmen within a year. Alain established his base of power at Nantes. See also below, 19E, 21G.

91 Flodoard adds, *Hist. Remensis Eccl.*, 4.26 (ed. Stratmann, 418), that the other bishops of the province of Reims, except for the bishops of Châlon-sur-Marne and Amiens, also participated in the consecration.

92 Otto I's chief rival for the kingship was his younger brother Henry.

93 There was an eclipse of the moon on 3-4 September 936; Liu and Fiala, *Canon of Lunar Eclipses*, 122, no. 5910.

94 Pope Leo VII had been cardinal priest of S. Sisto.

95 The joint military expedition of King Louis IV and Hugh the Great against Hugh the Black resulted in a division of the duchy of Burgundy between the two Hughs.

96 Hugh the Great was first styled Duke of the Franks, *dux Francorum*, in 936, which probably signified a position approximating that of a viceroy; see F.L. Ganshof, "À propos de ducs et de duchés au haut moyen âge," *Journal des savants* (Jan-Mar 1972) 13-24, esp. 15-16; Karl Ferdinand Werner, "La genèse des duchés en France et en Allemagne," in *Nascita dell'Europa ed Europa carolingia: un'equazione da verificare*, Settimane di Studio del Centro Italiano di Studi sull'Alto Medioevo, 27 (Spoleto: Presso la Sede del Centro, 1981) 175-207, esp. 197; Karl Ferdinand Werner, "Kingdom and principality in twelfth-century France," *The Medieval Nobility, Studies on the ruling classes of France and Germany from the sixth to the twelfth century*, ed. and trans. Timothy Reuter (Amsterdam, New York and Oxford: North Holland Publishing, 1978), originally published as "Königtum und Fürstentum des französischen 12. Jahrhunderts," *Probleme des 12. Jahrhunderts* (Sigmaringen: Jan Thorbecke Verlag, 1968) 177-225, 243-90, esp. 252. In that year of 936, King Louis IV issued a charter in which Hugh the Great was referred to as one "who in all our realms is second to us" ("qui est in omnibus regnis nostris secundus a nobis"), *Recueil des Actes de Louis IV, roi de France (936-954)*, ed. Maurice Prou and Philippe Lauer, Chartes et diplômes de France publiés par les soins de l'Académie des inscriptions et belles-lettres (Paris: C. Klincksieck, 1914) 10, no. 4.

Flodoard did not refer to Hugh the Great as duke until 943 (25B), that is, after the death of Count Heribert of Vermandois (25A), which probably reflected Flodoard's loyalty to Reims, which was under the domination of Count Heribert.

97 Rudolf II died 11 July 937 (Lauer, *Annales*, 68, n. 3); he had been elected king of Italy in 922, but Hugh of Arles was able to oust him from Italy and ca. 931 the two made a treaty whereby Rudolf II ceded his claims to Italy for the rule of the kingdom of Provence. The merger of the kingdoms of Transjurane Burgundy and Provence created the kingdom of Burgundy that was taken over by Conrad II of Germany in 1032.

98 Conrad the Peaceful (937-93) was eight or nine years old at his accession (Lauer, *Annales*, 68, n. 3).

99 Roger, count of Aouai, son of Count Roger of Laon and of Heiluidis, and half-brother of Raoul de Gouy (Lauer, *Annales*, 69, n. 2).

100 Ragebertus was a close relative, *consobrinus*, of Archbishop Artoldus, *Hist. Remensis Eccl.*, 4.26 (ed. Stratmann, 418).

101 Aethelstan was the nephew of Arnulf's mother Aelfthryth, the daughter of King Alfred, and was thus Arnulf's cousin.

102 Literally "the places of the Morini touching the sea" (*loca Morinorum mari contigua*); the classical Roman name for the inhabitants of western Flanders was Morini (Nicholas, *Medieval Flanders*, 20).

103 The battle of Trans (Lauer, *Annales*, 74, n. 4; Nora K. Chadwick, *Early Brittany* [Cardiff: University of Wales Press, 1969] 234).

104 Hugh the Great is referred to here as Albus, the White, which could be a corruption of *Abbas*, the abbot (Lauer, *Annales*, 74, n. 7). Hugh was the lay abbot of the monasteries of St-Martin of Tours, Marmoutier, St-Germain of Auxerre, Saint Denis, Morienval, Saint Riquier, St-Valéry and perhaps also of St-Aignan of Orléans, St-Germain-des-Prés and St-Maur des Fosses (McKitterick, *Frankish Kingdoms*, 314).

105 That is, Artoldus held the position of count of Reims. The charter to which Flodoard referred (and see *Hist. Remensis Eccl.* 4.27 [ed. Stratmann, 418]) is not extant, but is catalogued in *Recueil des Actes de Louis IV*, 37-8, no. 13.

106 No charter for this grant survives; see *Recueil des actes de Louis IV*, 38, no. 14.

107 Artoldus received both the monastery of St-Pierre at Avenay and St-Basle as compensation; Flodoard, *Hist. Remensis Eccl.*, 4.28 (ed. Stratmann, 419); Avenay is about 15 km south of Reims, close to Épernay, while St-Basle is about five km northeast of Avenay.

108 On his selection in 925, see above, 7G.

109 Flodoard recorded (*Hist. Remensis Eccl.*, 4.28, ed. Stratmann, 419-20) that Hugh had received minor orders at Reims, had been educated at Auxerre and then ordained deacon there by its bishop Guy, and in this year of 940 was made a priest by Bishop Guy of Soissons, three months after his return to Reims, now fifteen years after his initial election as bishop.

110 Flodoard's captivity lasted from 25 October 940 to 25 March 941 (Lauer, *Annales*, 78, n. 5). This was the second deprivation of his church holdings by Count Heribert; see above, 7G and n. In the *Hist. Remensis Eccl.*, 4.28 (ed. Stratmann, 420), Flodoard describes his loose custody ("sub custodia partim libera sum detentus") and ascribed the end of his captivity to the intercession of the Virgin Mary.

111 In modern Switzerland.

112 Count Arnold had been expelled from Douai by Lotharingian allies of Hugh the Great, *Hist. Remensis Eccl.*, 4.23 (Lauer, *Annales*, 81, n. 3).

113 The cathedral of Notre-Dame.

114 Son of Manasses I, count of Chaunois and of Autun, brother-in-law of Hugh the Black, duke of Burgundy, by his marriage to Hugh's sister Ermengard (Lauer, *Annales*, 81, n. 9).

115 Leader of the Northmen of Rouen.

116 Duke William Towhead of Aquitaine.

117 The leaders of the Bretons were Berengar, count of Rennes, Budic, count of Cornouaille, and Alain Barbetorte, count of Nantes (Lauer, *Annales*, 84-85, n. 9).

118 See above, 7B, 21C; Otho had been duke of Lotharingia since 939 or 940 (Lauer, *Annales*, 85, n. 2).

119 With the death of Heribert of Vermandois (25A), Flodoard now styles Hugh the

Great as duke of the Franks, a position he had held since 936.

120 On the different versions of the death of Heribert of Vermandois, see Lauer, *Louis IV d'Outre-Mer*, 94, 222-29.

121 Raoul might have been Louis IV's nephew (Lauer, *Annales*, 87, n. 4).

122 Heribert II of Vermandois had been married to Hugh the Great's sister Adele. Heribert's sons were Odo (died ca. 946), count of Amiens, Heribert the Elder (died 980/84), count of Omois, Robert (died after 967), count of Meaux and Châlons-sur-Saône, Adalbert (died 987), count of Vermandois, and Hugh (920-62), archbishop of Reims.

123 The *ducatus Franciae* was the administration of the *regnum* (duchy) of Francia, the region between the Loire and the Rhine (Ganshof, "À propos de ducs," 14-61; Werner, "La genèse," 180-83), and see above, 19B n. Lauer sees this as a regranting, or confirmation, of the position of Hugh as *dux Francorum* (*Louis IV d'Outre-Mer*, 108). Richer, *Historia*, 2.39 (ed. Latouche 1:188), stated that the king established Hugh as *dux* of all the Gauls, "Unde et eum rex omnium Galliarum ducem constituit."

124 Raymond-Pons III, count of Toulouse (923-50); sometime before 924, Gothia (see the glossary) passed into the hands of the counts of Toulouse (Jan Dhondt, *Études sur la naissance des principautés territoriales en France (IXe-Xe siècle)* [Bruges: De Tempel, 1948] 228.)

125 Probably Ragenoldus of Roucy (Lauer, *Annales*, 91, n. 4).

126 See above, 26A.

127 He died in 953; see Lauer, *Louis IV d'Outre-Mer*, 135, n. 4.

128 Theobald the Trickster, count of Tours. Originally viscount of Tours, he began taking the title of count around 940. In addition to the county of Tours, he also held the counties of Blois, Chartres and Châteaudun. He seems to have died at some time in the 970s, probably before 977 (see Jacques Boussard, "Les origines des comtés de Tours, Blois et Chartres," *Actes du 103e Congrès national de Sociétés savantes* [Paris: Bibliothèque Nationale, 1979] 85-112, esp. 90-93). He was the second husband of Liutgard, daughter of Heribert II of Vermandois (who was first married to William Longsword). On Theobald, see also Lauer, *Louis IV d'Outre-Mer*, p. 6, n. 3, and Yves Sassier, "Thibaud le Tricheur et Hugues le Grand," *Pays de Loire et Aquitaine de Robert le Fort aux premiers Capétiens*, ed. Olivier Guillot and Robert Favreau, *Mémoires de la Société des Antiquaires de l'Ouest*, 5th ser., 4 (1996) 145-57.

129 Heribert the Elder, son of Count Heribert II of Vermandois.

130 Ash Wednesday was on 19 February, while Easter was on 6 April.

131 Conrad the Red, who married Otto I's daughter Liutgard in 947; he was the great-grandfather of King Conrad III of Germany, 1024-39.

132 This is the first known instance of ergotism (or Saint Anthony's fire). Ergot is a fungus (Claviceps purpurea) that grows on cereal grasses, especially rye, and con-

tains a number of alkaloids, including lysergic acid, the principal component of
lysergic acid diethylamide (LSD), and even LSD itself. Those who eat bread produced from rye contaminated with ergot can experience strong hallucinogenic
episodes, with both rapturous and hellish visions. There is both gangrenous ergotism, in which the sufferer experiences burning sensations in the extremities due
to the constriction of arteries and veins, and convulsive ergotism, in which the
sufferer has muscles spasms and convulsions. See Mary Kilbourne Matossian, *Poisons of the Past* (New Haven and London, 1989) 9-14, and "Mold Poisoning and
Population Growth in England and France, 1750-1850," *Journal of Economic History*
44 (1984): 673-74.

133 Edmund I, 939-46, son of Edward the Elder, and thus uncle of Louis IV and
brother-in-law of both Hugh the Great and King Otto I of Germany.

134 The sons of Heribert II of Vermandois and Adele, Hugh's sister.

135 Edmund I was assassinated on 26 May.

136 Adele, the daughter of Heribert II and Adele (sister of Hugh the Great), was married to Arnulf of Flanders (Lauer, *Annales*, 102, n. 5).

137 A daughter of Count Heribert II.

138 Future archbishop of Cologne.

139 The bishops of Metz, Toul, and Verdun.

140 The bishops of Soissons, Châlons-sur-Marne, Vermand, Arras, Cambrai, Tournai,
Senlis, Beauvais, Amiens, Thérouanne, Boulogne, and Laon.

141 The canons "of the council of Carthage" came from different councils of
Carthage but for the most part were from those of 419, which were included in
the early sixth-century collection of canons of church councils and decretals of
fifth-century popes made by Dionysius Exiguus in the early sixth century, known
variously as the *Liber Canonum*, *Collectio Dionysiana*, or *Collectio Dionysio-Hadriana*
(an eighth-century revised edition). The canons of the Council of Carthage are in
A Select Library of Nicene and Post-Nicene Fathers of the Christian Church, ed. Philip
Schaff and Henry Wace, 2nd ser. 17, ed. Henry R. Percival (Edinburgh: T&T
Clark, Edinburgh; Grand Rapids, MI: Eerdmans, 1991) 438-510.

142 "Teutisca lingua," which is the same phrase ("Teudisca lingua") used three times
by Nithard in his *Histories* to describe the Strasbourg oaths taken in the German
language by Charles the Bald in 842; for the Latin text, see *Quellen zur karolingis-
chen Reichsgeschichte*, ed. Reinhold Rau, vol. 1, Fontes ad Historiam Regni Francorum Aevi Karolini Illustrandam (Darmstadt: Wissenschaftliche Buchgesellschaft
E.V., 1955) 3.5; for an English translation, see *Carolingian Chronicles*, trans. Bernhard Walter Scholz, with Barbara Rogers (Ann Arbor: University of Michigan
Press, 1972) 161-62. On the language spoken by Louis IV and Otto I at this meeting, see Paul Christophersen, "The Spoken Word in International Contacts in
Carolingian Europe," *NOWELE* [*North-western European Language Evolution*] 20
(1992): 53-64.

143 See above, 30A.

144 That is, according to the canons of the Council of Carthage; see above, 30A and n.

145 Many of these are popes whose decrees were included in the collection of canon law by Dionysius Exiguus (see above, 30A, n.): Innocent (I, 407-17), Zosimus (417-18), Boniface (I, 418-22), Celestine (I, 422-32), Leo (I, 440-61), Symmachus (498-514).

146 Evidence of Flodoard's participation in the council.

147 Hugh was able to escape in the confusion; see Richer, *Historia*, 2.83 (ed. Latouche 1:268-70).

148 The cathedral.

149 That is, the episcopal quarter, clearly distinguished here from the *urbs*, the city itself.

150 *Vallavit*, that is, surrounding the fortification with a ditch, with the excavated material thrown up to form a rampart, see above 30N.

151 Literally, the bishop of the Morini (*episcopus Morinensis*); on the Morini, see above, 21D and n.

152 *Morinensis*, see n. 151 above.

153 Named Sylvester according to Richer, *Historia*, 2.82 (ed. Latouche 1:266).

154 Perhaps the bishop of Osnabrück (Lauer, *Annales*, 119, n. 3).

155 Flodoard returns to the title *comes* for Hugh the Great, rather than *princeps* or *dux*, because of Hugh's excommunication and the actions that prompted it.

156 The monastery of Fulda was reconsecrated on 1 November 948.

157 Louis IV's son Louis died at the age of 5, shortly before the death of Louis IV (Lauer, *Annales*, 121, n. 1); see below, 36B.

158 Richer, *Historia*, 2.82 (ed. Latouche 1:268), states that Rorico was Louis's brother by a concubine and was a man given to knowledge; he also was a royal notary (Lauer, *Louis IV d'Outre-Mer*, 196).

159 Son of Count Heribert II of Vermandois.

160 There is a village of Ste-Marie-à-Py (Lauer, *Annales*, 126, n. 2), about 35 km west of Reims.

161 Raoul was King Louis's relative (Lauer, *Louis IV d'Outre-Mer*, 208).

162 Only Flodoard mentions the siege of Prague. Widukind (*Widukindi Monachi Corbeinsis Rerum Gestarum Saxonicarum Libri Tres*, ed. G. Waitz and K.A. Kehr, 5th ed. [Hannover: Hahnsche Buchhandlung, 1935] 3.8) speaks of the siege of Nimburg, east of Prague (Lauer, *Annales*, 128, n. 1).

163 See above, 32B.

164 *Princeps*; Berengar II (king of Italy 950-61) had been count of Ivrea and was grandson of Berengar I, king of Italy (888-925) and emperor (915-24).

165 Lothair died on 22 November, and Berengar was crowned king, along with his son Adalbert, on 15 December.

166 Count Frederick of Bar was engaged to Hugh's daughter Beatrice (Lauer, *Louis IV d'Outre-Mer*, 214 and n. 3). For their marriage, see 36E.

167 Ash Wednesday was on 12 February, with Easter falling on 30 March.

168 Probably Ragenarius III of Hainault.

169 Erluinus had died in 945 (Lauer, *Annales*, 131, n. 8).

170 Son of Erluinus, count of Ponthieu.

171 Perhaps St-Valery-sur-Somme (Lauer, *Annales*, 132, n. 2 and Lauer, *Louis IV d'Outre-Mer*, 219).

172 This is Eadgifu, daughter of King Edward the Elder of England and wife of King Charles the Simple. Richer, *Historia*, 2.6 (ed. Latouche 1:136), names her as Ethgiva. On forms of her name, see Lauer, *Louis IV d'Outre-Mer*, 9, n. 4.

173 Sons of Heribert II of Vermandois.

174 Notre-Dame de Laon.

175 Sons of Count Heribert II of Vermandois.

176 His identity is uncertain, but perhaps he was the son of Waleran, count of Vexin, Amiens, Valois, and Dreux (Lauer, *Annales*, 134, n. 3).

177 Son of Count Heribert II of Vermandois.

178 See Lauer, *Louis IV d'Outre-Mer*, 223.

179 Lent ran from 16 February to 3 April in 953; Mid-Lent Sunday (Laetare Sunday) is the fourth Sunday in Lent, which was 13 March 953.

180 The future emperor Otto II, 973-83.

181 Liudolf had been named Otto I's successor in 946.

182 The later Charles of Lorraine.

183 On his birth, see above, 30Q.

184 Louis IV died 10 September 954 (Lauer, *Louis IV d'Outre-Mer*, 231).

185 See above, 33B and n.

186 Son of Count Heribert II of Vermandois.

187 Count of Omois, son of Heribert II of Vermandois.

188 Count of Meaux and Troyes.

189 Alberic died 31 August; Octavian was his illegitimate son.

190 Agapitus died December 955. Octavian, only eighteen years old, took the papal name John XII (16 December 955-14 May 964), being the second pope to do so, the first being John II in 533.

191 Boleslav I, duke, or king (see 37D) of Bohemia (929-967); on the Sarmatians (Sarmatae) as Slavs, see 6F.

192 The battle of the Lechfeld, 10 August.

193 *Sarmatae*, that is, Slavs; see above, 6F.

194 Flodoard here refers to Boleslav as king (*rex*); Widukind of Corvey, *Res gestae Saxonicae*, also styles Boleslav "king of the Bohemians," 3.8, 69.

195 16 or 17 June.

196 Bovo died in 947, see 29B above.

197 The cathedral of Notre-Dame.

198 Archbishop of Cologne and duke of Lotharingia.

199 Ragenarius III of Hainault.

200 Archbishop of Cologne and duke of Lotharingia.

201 Sons of Count Heribert II of Vermandois.

202 *Sarmatae*, the Slavs; see above, 6F.

203 Presumably King Lothair and Hugh Capet, Odo and Odo-Henry, sons of Hugh
     the Great.

204 See above, 40B n.

205 Ash Wednesday fell on 16 February, with Easter on 3 April.

206 The cathedral of Notre-Dame.

207 Count of Meaux and Troyes, son of Count Heribert II of Vermandois.

208 Son of Ragenarius III Long-Neck of Hainault (Lauer, *Annales*, p. 264).

209 Son of Count Heribert II of Vermandois.

210 Hugh Capet and his brother Odo were first cousins of King Lothair, being sons of
     Lothair's aunt Hadwig.

211 See above, 41B.

212 Ash Wednesday was on 20 February, and Easter was on 7 April.

213 The other sons of Count Heribert II of Vermandois.

214 Otto was crowned emperor 2 February 962.

215 Perhaps at Isle-sur-Marne (Lauer, *Annales*, 151, n. 4; Richer, *Historia*, ed. Latouche
     2:24-25, n. 2).

216 John XII. However, the deposed Archbishop Hugh died shortly after this synod;
     see Ferdinand Lot, *Les derniers Carolingiens, Lothaire, Louis V, Charles de Lorraine,
     954–991* (Paris: Émile Bouillon, 1891; repr. Geneva: Slatkine Reprints; Paris: Hon-
     oré Champion, 1975) 40-41 and n., and Richer, *Historia*, 3.17 (ed. Latouche 2:25).

217 *Servus* can refer to a slave, a serf, or a servant.

218 This perhaps is Arnulf, count of Boulogne, the son of Count Arnulf's brother
     Adalolf, count of Boulogne and Ternois (Nicholas, *Medieval Flanders*, 42).

219 This recognition of royal authority made King Lothair the guardian of Count
     Arnulf I's grandson, Arnulf II, and thus assured his succession in the face of the
     previous hostility between Arnulf I and his nephew Arnulf (see Nicholas, *Medieval
     Flanders*, 43).

220 Note the participation of Flodoard.

221 A canon of the cathedral of Metz; Richer, *Historia*, 3.18 (ed. Latouche 2:26);
     Odelricus was from a Lotharingian family claiming descent from Bishop Arnulf of
     Metz, a seventh-century ancestor of the Carolingians; see Lot, *Les derniers Car-
     olingiens*, 40.

222 Sons of Count Heribert II of Vermandois.

223 Count of Omois, son of Heribert II of Vermandois.

224 Otto-Henry, duke of Burgundy; Otto (Oddo in Flodoard's text) was at first a

monk but upon the death of his brother Odo, he left the monastic life to become duke of Burgundy and adopted the name of his mother's father, King Henry I of Germany (see Andrew W. Lewis, *Royal Succession in Capetian France: Studies on Familial Order and the State* [Cambridge, MA, and London: Harvard University Press, 1981] 11).

225 The future Charles of Lorraine.

226 "Ad imperii regenda gubernacula."

227 John XII quarreled with Emperor Otto and plotted with the Magyars and with Adalbert, son of Berengar, Emperor Otto's former rival for Italy. At the appearance of Otto (1 October 963), John XII fled Rome for Tivoli and was deposed as pope by a Roman synod on 4 December 963. Emperor Otto then arranged the election of Leo VIII, a papal notary, who was not a cleric, and he was consecrated pope on 6 December 963. At the death of John XII (14 May 964), the Romans did not accept Leo VIII, but instead elected Benedict V as pope (see the following three notes). Emperor Otto entered Rome and reinstated Leo VIII (23 June 964). Leo died on 1 March 965.

228 The elevation to the papacy of John XIII, who had been bishop of Narnia in Umbria, was on 1 October 965, following the death of Pope Leo VIII (1 March 965).

229 Octavian (John XII) died on 14 May 964.

230 Actually Leo VIII was restored.

231 Upon the death of John XII in May 964, Benedict V was chosen pope by the people and clergy of Rome over the objections of Emperor Otto, who considered Leo VIII still to be pope. Otto besieged and took Rome and arranged for Benedict's condemnation and deposition (June 964), with Leo VIII restored as pope. Benedict was then exiled to Hamburg, where he died on 4 July 966. Leo VIII then died on 1 March 965 and was succeeded as pope by John XIII (1 October 965-6 September 972).

232 Emma was the daughter of King Lothair and Adelaid, and thus the step-daughter of King Otto I of Germany and niece of King Conrad of Burgundy.

GLOSSARY

Abbatia: abbotship, the office of abbot of a monastery, or also all of the rights, lands and possessions of the monastery; or even the monastery itself.

Castellum, pl. *castella*: a fortification consisting of a single tower or keep, often surrounded by a curtain wall. The tower, if intended to be permanent, was usually constructed of stone, but temporary *castella* were generally built of wood. A curtain wall was usually, but not always, of wood. A *castellum* was usually smaller than a *castrum*.

Castrum, pl. *castra*: a fortification, often very large and well constructed of stone (for example, at Laon), with a central inner fortification and stone outer walls with towers. Some *castra* were larger than *urbes*.

Civitas, pl. *civitates*: a term of many related meanings. It could refer to an administrative district, synonymous with *pagus*. These districts were developed during the Roman Empire and were generally coterminous with the diocese (and the term could refer specifically to a diocese or even to the episcopal district in the diocesan capital) as well as with the modern French *département*. Sometimes the *civitas* was synonymous with the *urbs*, which was the center or capital of the *civitas*. Usually the head of the *civitas* was the count.

Fidelis, pl. *fideles*: a man who recognized himself to be the loyal or faithful supporter of another person whom he recognized as his own superior. Becoming a *fidelis* entailed taking an oath of faithfulness to one's superior, or lord (*dominus* or *senior* in Latin).

Franks: the *Franci*, pl: inhabitants of Francia (see below); Flodoard's *Franci* were not the same as the Franks of the Merovingian and earlier Carolingian periods, and these Franks should not be understood as "French" in the modern sense.

Francia: roughly the region bounded by the Rhine, the English Channel and the Loire river. To Flodoard, Aquitaine and Burgundy were not in Francia, while Lotharingia was sometimes included in it and sometimes not. Francia, therefore, is only one region of modern France and should not be confused with it.

Gothia: the coastal region of southern France, between the Rhône and the Pyrenees.

Marchio: a marquis or margrave, that is, the head of a mark or march, that is, a border or frontier region; the *marchio* held virtual viceregal authority in his territory.

Munitio, pl. *munitiones*: a fortification in general, the specific type of which can be ascertained only from the specific context.

Nepos, pl. *nepotes*: an ambiguous Latin term that could refer to a nephew, grandson, cousin or a close relative in general.

Oppidum, pl. *oppida*: a fortification, generally describing a *castrum* (see above), sometimes a *castellum* and at times even an *urbs*. *Oppida* are generally of stone but there could be exceptions.

Pagus, pl. *pagi*: a term with a wide variety of meanings to designate a district or region; in Flodoard, it is generally synonymous with "county" but can also be synonymous with *civitas*.

Pallium: a white woolen stole, usually with six black crosses, worn around the neck, given by popes to archbishops as symbols of their position and authority.

Placitum, pl. *placita*: a meeting or a document stemming from such a meeting. Often the term is used for a judicial, public, or governmental meeting.

Portus: a settlement of merchants which could serve as a trading center.

Praesidium, pl. *praesidia*: usually a fortified area within a larger fortification, that is a citadel or redoubt.

Princeps, pl. *principes*: literally first man or leading man. Flodoard uses the term for a very wide range of figures, for kings (Henry I of Germany and Boleslav of the Slavs), dukes and counts (William Longsword of the Northmen, Hugh the Great, Arnulf of Flanders), as well as in a general way for magnates of a kingdom or region.

Urbs, pl. *urbes*: the secular administrative capital of a *civitas* or *pagus*, which was usually headed by a count, as well as seat of the diocesan administration of a bishopric.

Villa, pl. *villae*: an agricultural administrative unit, which was usually an estate with harvests divided between the lord of the estate and the agricultural workers who labored on the lands; a *villa* was also the administrative center of such an estate.

MAPS

Map 1. The World of Flodoard's *Annals*

Map 2. Reims and its Surrounding Region

Map 3. The Political Boundaries of the West Frankish Kingdom *ca.* 1000

Map 4. The German Kingdom in the Tenth Century

GENEALOGIES

1. Descendants of Charlemagne

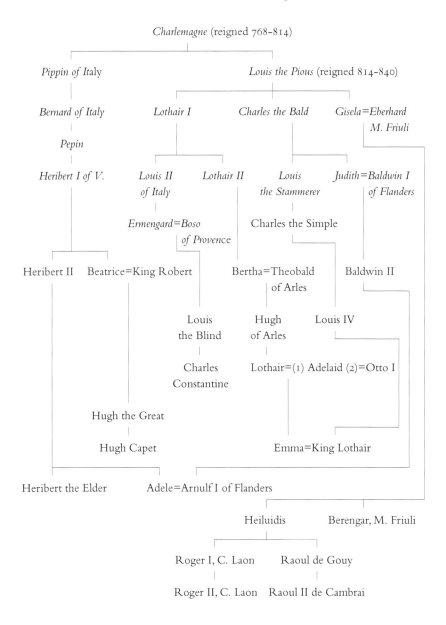

Charlemagne (reigned 768-814)

Pippin of Italy   *Louis the Pious* (reigned 814-840)

Bernard of Italy   *Lothair I*   *Charles the Bald*   *Gisela=Eberhard*
                                                          M. Friuli

Pepin

Heribert I of V.   *Louis II*   *Lothair II*   *Louis*   *Judith=Baldwin I*
                     of Italy   *the Stammerer*   *of Flanders*

Ermengard=Boso   Charles the Simple
of Provence

Heribert II   Beatrice=King Robert   Bertha=Theobald   Baldwin II
                                           of Arles

Louis   Hugh   Louis IV
the Blind   of Arles

Charles   Lothair=(1) Adelaid (2)=Otto I
Constantine

Hugh the Great

Hugh Capet   Emma=King Lothair

Heribert the Elder   Adele=Arnulf I of Flanders

Heiluidis   Berengar, M. Friuli

Roger I, C. Laon   Raoul de Gouy

Roger II, C. Laon Raoul II de Cambrai

(*Names in italics are not in the text of Flodoard's* Annals)

91

2. Tenth-Century Carolingian Kings of the West Franks

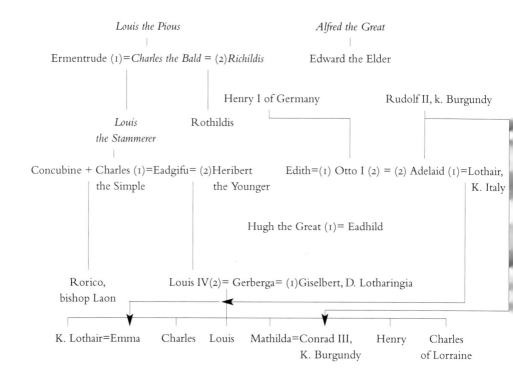

3. The Robertians

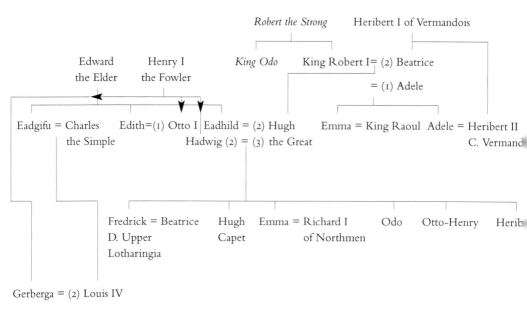

4. The House of Vermandois

Genealogy 1

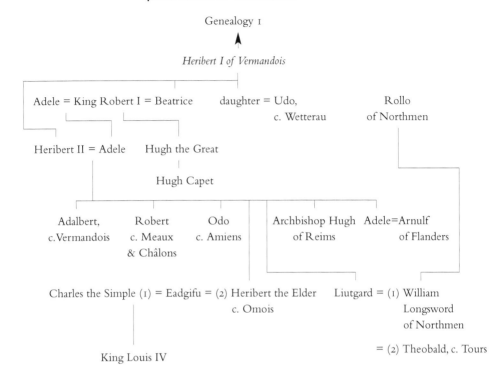

Heribert I of Vermandois

Adele = King Robert I = Beatrice   daughter = Udo,   Rollo
                                              c. Wetterau   of Northmen

Heribert II = Adele   Hugh the Great

Hugh Capet

Adalbert,   Robert   Odo   Archbishop Hugh Adele=Arnulf
c. Vermandois   c. Meaux   c. Amiens   of Reims   of Flanders
            & Châlons

Charles the Simple (1) = Eadgifu = (2) Heribert the Elder   Liutgard = (1) William
                                          c. Omois   Longsword
                                                      of Northmen

                                                      = (2) Theobald, c. Tours

King Louis IV

5. Saxon Kings of Germany

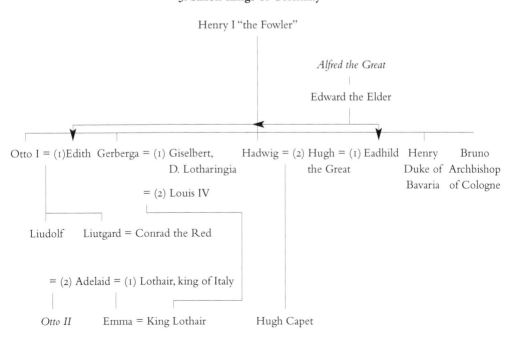

Henry I "the Fowler"

Alfred the Great

Edward the Elder

Otto I = (1)Edith Gerberga = (1) Giselbert,   Hadwig = (2) Hugh = (1) Eadhild Henry   Bruno
                        D. Lotharingia   the Great   Duke of Archbishop
                                                      Bavaria of Cologne
                = (2) Louis IV

Liudolf   Liutgard = Conrad the Red

= (2) Adelaid = (1) Lothair, king of Italy

Otto II   Emma = King Lothair   Hugh Capet

93

6. Descendants of Alfred the Great of England

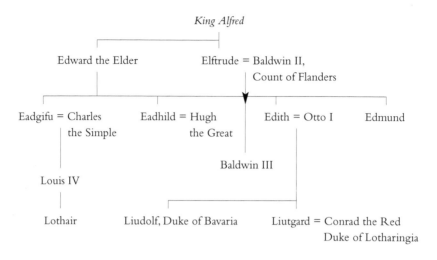

7. The Counts of Flanders

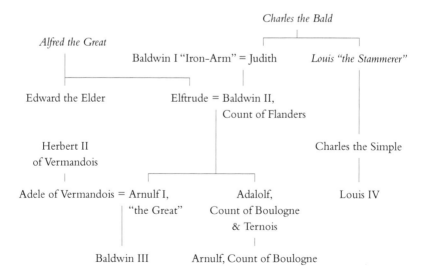

8. Dukes of Burgundy

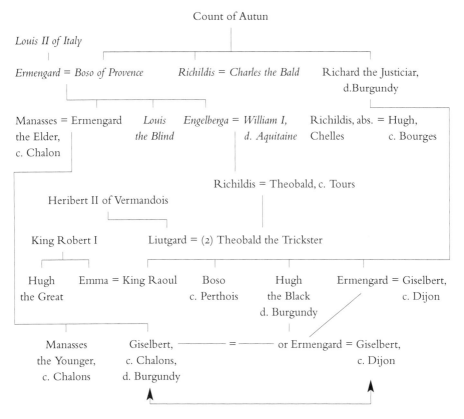

9. Kings of Upper Burgundy

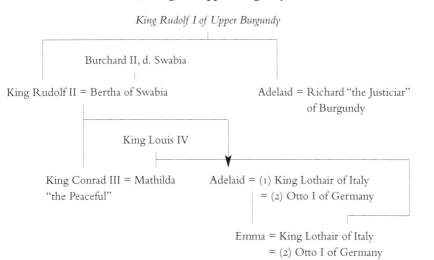

INDEX

Parentheses indicate persons referred to but not named explicitly in the text. French places are identified in the customary modern style listing département, commune, canton and arrondissement, as given by Lauer in the index of *Les Annales de Flodoard*. The number and letter (e. g., 3A) refer to the subdivisions of the translated text of Flodoard.

John, bishop of Pavia 6D
John X, pope xxv, 4A, 5M, 10A, 10B, 11C
John XI, pope 15A, 18C
John XII, pope (Octavian) xix, xxvi, 36H, (44D), 44H, 47E
John XIII, pope 47E
Joscelin, bishop of Langres 7A
Judicaël Beranger, count of Rennes, see Berengar
Judith, daughter of Charles the Bald xx
Jura 17A, 19E, 22E, 33H
    see also Cisalpine Gaul, Upper Burgundy
Juziers (Seine-et-Marne, arr. de Mantes, cant. de Limay; map 2) *villa* of 4H

la Fère (Aisne, arr. de Laon; map 2), *castrum, munitio* of 40A
Landricus, brother of Arnold of Douai 23F
Langres (maps 1, 3) 18B
    see also Bishop Joscelin
Lantbertus, son of Ragenarius of Hainault 42A
Laon (maps 1, 2, 3) xvi, xviii, 3A, 3E, 4C, 4D, 5E, 5J, 5K, 8A, 9C, 10A, 13F, 13H,
    17A, 17C, 18A, 20B, 21E, 22A, 22C, 22D, 22E, 23F, 24A, 27A, 28E, 28G,
    30F, 30K, 31A, 31D, 31E, 32A, 32C, 32E, 33G, 34B, 34D, 35C, 36B, 36F,
    41B, 42C, 43B, 47B
    bishopric of 18B
    castellum of 9C
    castrum of 5E, 21E, 28E, 28G, 30F, 31D
    church of St. Vincent 30K
    county of 9A, 23F
    mint of 22A
    Mount of 3A, 3E
    oppidum of 31D
    pagus of 4C, 9B, 36A, 40A
    see also bishops Adelelmus, Gosbert, Ingramnus, Raoul I, Raoul II, Rorico
Lavannes (Marne; map 2), *villa* of 22F
Lechfeld, battle of xxiv, xxvii, 37C
Le Mans (maps 1, 3) 6A
Leo VII, pope x, 18C
Letoldus, of Mâcon, Burgundian count 33A
Liège (maps 1, 2, 4), see Bishop Baldricus
Liesdac, bishop of Ribe in Denmark 30E
Limoges (maps 1, 3), *pagus* of 12A
Lioptacus, bishop of Ribe in Denmark 30E
Liudulfus, legate of King Otto I 30P, 30Q

Montmartre 26F
pagus of 4H, 26G, 27H
Passau (maps 1, 4), see Bishop Adalbert
Paul, blind man 16B
Pavia (map 1) 6D, 33H, 34A, 34B, 47E
  civitas of 6D
  synod of 44H
  urbs of 6D
  see also Bishop John
Péronne (maps 1, 2), *munitio* of 6A, 11D, 14D, 16D
Pierrepont (Aisne, arr. de Laon, canton de Marle; map 2), *castrum* of, 20B
  munitio of 22D, 22F, 31A
pilgrimages 2D, 3B, 5M, 11E, 18D, 21G, 33I
placitum 6E, 7B
plague 6J, 9A, 16E, 38B
Poitiers (maps 1, 3) 37B
Poitou, *pagus* of (map 3) 42B
Ponthieu (map 1) xx, (8A), (29F), (39B)
  see also counts Erluinus, Hilgaudus, Roger
Ponthion (Marne, arr. de Vitry-le-François, cant. de Thiéblemont; map 2)
  34D
popes, see Agapitus II, Benedict V, John X, John XI, John XII, John XIII, Leo
  VII, Marinus, Stephen VIII, Stephen IX
Poppo, bishop of Würzburg 30E
Porcien, *pagus* of (map 3) 8A, 15B, 23F, 31E
Prague (map 4) 32D
Prüm, abbey of (maps 1, 4) (2C)
le Puy, stream (map 2) 31H

Ragamfridus, bishop of Vercelli 6D
Ragebertus 20A
Ragembaldus, monk, bishop of Amiens 31B, 32C
Ragenardus, viscount of Auxerre, brother of Manasses I, count of Dijon 6B,
  6F, 6H
Ragenarius [Rainier II], brother of Gislebert of Lorraine 6C, 10C
Ragenarius, *fidelis* of King Louis IV, brother of Raoul 26D
Ragenarius, count (probably Rainier III of Hainault) 33C, 33C, 35B, 36A,
  38C, 39B
  children of 38C
Ragenoldus (count of Roucy) 26A, 26F, 27C, 29I, 30N, 31D, 31E, 32A, 32D,
  34C, 34D, 35D, 36F, 37B, 48B
  soldiers of 36G

Ragenold, the *princeps* of the Northmen xxi, 5H, 6G, 6H, 7A

Rag(e)inardus, see Ragenardus, viscount of Auxerre

Ramfridus, bishop of Vercelli 6D

Ramnulf, count of Poitou xv, xxii

Raoul, archdeacon, bishop of Noyon at Compiègne 32B, 32F

Raoul I, bishop of Laon 3A

Raoul II, bishop of Laon 18B, 20B, 21E, 24E, 30E, 30G, 30H, 30K, 30O, 30P, 30Q

Raoul, brother of Roger 25D

Raoul de Gouy, count, stepson of Roger of Laon, son of Heluidis 5H, 7F, 8E

Raoul, *fidelis* of King Louis IV, brother of Ragenarius 26C

Raoul, duke of the Burgundians, king of Franks ix, xvi-xvii, xxi-xxii, xxiv-xxv, xxvii-xxviii, 4C, 5F, 5G, 5I, 5J, 5K, 5L, 5M, 6A, 6B, 6C, 6E, 6F, 6H, 7A, 7B, 7E, 7F, 8A, 8C, 9A, 9C, 10A, 10D, 12A, 12B, 13E, 13F, 13H, 14A, 14B, 14D, 15B, 16A, 16C, 16D, 17A, 17B, 17C, 17D, 18A

Raoul, son of Raoul de Gouy 25A

Raymond (Raymond-Pons III, count of Toulouse, *princeps* of Gothia) xxii, 5B, 14D, 26A

Regensburg (maps 1, 4), see Bishop Michael

Reimboldus, bishop of Speyer 30E

Reims (maps 1, 2, 3) vii-xii, xvii-xviii, 1, 2A, 2B, 2D, 3A, 4D, 4E, 5J, 5M, 6I, 7F, 8B, 8D, 9A, 10A, 10D, 12C, 13F, 13H, (15C), 16B, 16E, 22B, 22C, 22E, 23D, 23E, 24B, 25D, 27B, 27C, 28G, 29A, 29D, 29G, 30A, 31B, 31E, 34D, 35A, 36B, 36G, 37E, 38E, 41C

    bishopric of 44A, 44C

    church of 2B, 4C, 7A, 7E, 10B, 20A, 21G, 22A, 24B, 29I, 30N, 31A, 31B, 31D, 38C, 40A, 42A, 45A, 46C, 48B

    villae of 4C, 4D

    church of St. Mary 6I, 12C, 13C, 16B, 23E, 32E, 39A, 41C

    churches of St. Denis and Tedulfus 13C

    church of St Hilary 16B

    county of 22A

    diocese of 2A, 4D, 7G, 9C, 22B, 23D, 25C, 25D, 26F, 29J, 30A, 30I, 44A, 44D

    gate of Mars 16B

    monastery of St. Peter 2D

    monastery of Saint-Rémi 4E

    pagus 1, 13F, 22D, 36A

    province of Reims 23D, 24A, 24E, 30A, 30G

    territory of 35D

    urbs of 2D, 4D

    see also archbishops Artoldus, Heriveus, Hugh, Odelricus, Seulfus

relics 4H

READINGS IN MEDIEVAL CIVILIZATIONS AND CULTURES
Series Editor: Paul Edward Dutton

"Readings in Medieval Civilizations and Cultures is in my opinion the most useful series being published today."
—William C. Jordan, Princeton University